Encyclopedia of the Worlds of Doctor Who
E–K

Text copyright © David Saunders, 1989
Illustrations copyright © Tony Clark, 1989

All rights reserved. No part of this publication may be reproduced, stored in a retrieval system, or transmitted, in any form or by any means electronic, mechanical, photocopying, recording or otherwise, without the prior permission of the copyright owner.

Phototypeset by York House Typographic Ltd., Hanwell, London W7
Printed and bound by MacLehose & Partners Ltd., Portsmouth for the publishers Piccadilly Press Ltd.,
5 Canfield Place, London NW6 3BT

British Library Cataloguing in Publication Data

Saunders, David
   Encyclopedia of the Worlds of Doctor Who. E-K
   1. Children's television drama series in
   English: Doctor Who
   I. Title II. Clark, Tony
   791.45'72

ISBN 1-85340-039-4

David Saunders is British and lives in London. He is a librarian who has followed *Doctor Who* since its inception. From 1980 – 1985 he was Coordinator of the Doctor Who Appreciation Society. He has written for 'Doctor Who Magazine' and contributed to the science-fiction orientated periodical 'Starburst'.

Tony Clark is a young recently-graduated illustrator who has also been a Doctor Who fan for many years. This is his second book for Piccadilly Press.

Encyclopedia of the Worlds of Doctor Who
E–K
David Saunders
Illustrated by Tony Clark

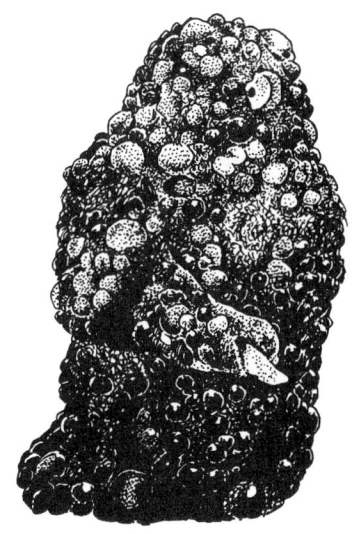

By arrangement with BBC Books, a division of BBC Enterprises Ltd
DOCTOR WHO is a registered trade mark
of the British Broadcasting Corporation

Piccadilly Press · London

To the memory of my mother, Mary, this volume is reciprocally and respectfully dedicated.

FOREWORD

In working on the second volume of the *Encyclopedia of the Worlds of Doctor Who* I have taken into account what lessons I learnt while compiling the first . . . Inevitably some errors crept into that volume and several omissions were made. It has been decided that any corrections for the series will be included at the end of the sixth volume which will primarily update the entries by covering the travels of the Seventh Doctor. One point which it is important to make is that in the printing of the Story Table two codes became interchanged: in the listing of stories for the Eighteenth Season that for *Meglos* should read 5Q whilst that for *State of Decay* should be 5P.

I should like to thank all those listed in the first volume for their assistance on this project and particularly Stephen James Walker, John Nathan-Turner, Deanne Holding, Nigel Robinson, Michael Smallman and Jan Vincent-Rudzki for their help in compiling the second and, of course, Tony Clark.

DAVID SAUNDERS
September 1988

E

Wyatt Earp

E=MC³
An equation used in the extra-temporal physics of the time vortex, mentioned by the Master. (OOO)

E-SPACE
A small universe into which the TARDIS was drawn (5R) through a Charged Vacuum Emboitment and from which it eventually escaped (5S).

EAG 113H
The registration number of Mike Yates' car at the time he was staying at the meditation centre in Mummerset. (ZZZ)

EAGLE
The aeroplane sent to bomb the coach containing Autons, driven by Rex Farrell. Its mission was aborted with the arrival of the Third Doctor, Jo and the Master. (EEE)

EAGLE
The call sign of the guerilla task force from the 22nd century led by Anat. (KKK)

THE EARP FAMILY
The Earp brothers, Wyatt and Virgil, helped by Doc Holliday, took on the Clanton family who had killed the

youngest Earp brother, Warren. The First Doctor became embroiled in the situation which culminated in the gunfight at the OK Corral outside Tombstone, Arizona in 1881. (Z)

EARTH

Our planet has in the course of history been affected by the Jagaroth (5H), the Cybermen (6B), the Fendahl (4X), the Daemons (JJJ), the Osirans (4G) and the Exxilons (XXX). It is strategic to the plans of the Sontarans (UUU, 4B, 6W), the Daleks (K, KKK, 6P) and the Cybermen (DD, HH, VV, 6T) and many other races which have, or will attempt to attack or dominate us. These include Axons (GGG), Chameleons (KK), Kraals (4J), Nestenes (AAA, EEE), Silurians and Sea Devils (BBB, LLL, 6L) and Zygons (4F) in this century and Ice Warriors (XX) and Vervoids (7C) in the ensuing ones while individuals and intelligences will/have attempt(ed) to do so also (GG, NN, PP, QQ, RR, 4G, 6M) as have computers (BB, TTT).

The first intelligent life on the planet was reptilian (BBB, LLL, 6L) but Man, helped by the intervention of several alien races, firmly became the dominant species. This holds true on at least one other-dimensional parallel world (DDD) but not on our physical twin, Mondas, now destroyed (DD).

After a further Ice Age (OO) and World Wars (4S) it is doomed to be affected by solar flares (4C) and most of the population will migrate to other colonies, e.g. Vulcan (EE), Uxarieus (HHH), Solos (NNN), Gal Sec (4B), Titan (4T) and Frontios (6N) or settle on Refusis II (X). The Earth, thought to burn up, will in fact be torn out of orbit by the Time Lords and moved some two light years away and re-named Ravolox (7C).

By Gallifreyan standards it is classed a level 5 civilisation (5H) and is a planet for which the Doctor has a particular affinity to judge from the number of visits his TARDIS has made to it. It is to Earth that he was banished by his own people during his period of exile (ZZ) and that planet from which many of his travelling companions originate.

EARTH COUNCIL

The government of Earth in the thirtieth century at the time of the pending independence of Solos. (NNN)

EARTHLING
The Earthman abducted as part of Meglos' plan to take over the Prion planetary system. (5Q)

ECKERSLEY
An Earth mining engineer who became an agent of Galaxy Five and allied himself with Ice Lord Azaxyr to supply Peladonian trisilicate to his employers. He was killed in a struggle with Aggedor. (YYY)

EDAL
The captain who served the Elders on the planet of *The Savages*. (AA)

EDEN
A planet visited by Tryst's expedition, and from which the Mandrells originate. (5K)

The Planet Eden

EDGEWORTH, Professor
The name adopted by the Time Lord Azmael when he became ruler of Joconda. (6S)

EDITH
The wife of Wulnoth and one of the Saxon villagers encountered by the First Doctor in 1066. She was assaulted by Viking raiders. (S)

EDU
A bandit of simple nature on the planet Chloris. (5G)

EDWARD VII
The British monarch whom the Doctor mentions he has met. (DDD)

EDWARD OF WESSEX
A Norman lord whose castle, where he lived with his wife Eleanor, was coveted by Irongron. (UUU)

EDWARDES
The communications officer on the *Hyperion III*. He was electrocuted by the Vervoids. (7C)

EDWARDS, Squire
The 17th century Cornish magistrate who was secretly one of *The Smugglers*. (CC)

EELEK
The ambitious deputy leader of the Council of the Gonds. (WW)

EINSTEIN, Albert
The twentieth century German scientist whom the Doctor mentions he has met. (5C)

EIRAK
The watch-commander of the Vanir on Terminus. (6G)

Squire Edwards

EL AKIR
A scar-faced, ruthless Saracen Emir. He was stabbed by Haroun in vengeance for all the cruelty the Saracen had wrought on his family. (P)

EL ALAMEIN
The battle during World War II which the Doctor mentions he has witnessed. (LLL)

THE ELDERS
The most senior caste of the Sensorites on the Sense-Sphere. (G)

THE ELDERS
The cannibalistic faction which ruled on the planet of *The Savages*. (AA)

THE ELDERS
Members of the ruling council in Atlantis at the time of the Third Doctor's visit there. (OOO).

THE ELDERS
The leaders among the Sarns who worshipped Logar. (6Q)

ELDRAD
A scientist of the planet Kastria and a silicon-based life form. Outlawed on his home planet, he escaped his sentence of complete obliteration and was stranded on Earth where, with the aid of nuclear energy, he regenerated himself, at first with a female body patterned on Sarah-Jane. With the aid of the Fourth Doctor he returned to his home planet to find it deserted and so vowed to rule Earth instead. However he was tricked by the Doctor and fell into a chasm. (4N)

ELDRED
One of the Saxon villagers encountered by the First Doctor in 1066. He was wounded in a skirmish with Viking raiders. (S)

ELDRED, Daniel
The Professor of Rocketry who ran a space museum in the 22nd century. (XX)

ELEANOR OF WESSEX
The wife of Edward of Wessex. (UUU)

ELENA
One of the ground staff of the Interplanetary Pursuit Squadron. (6S)

ELGIN
A security guard at the Nunton Experimental Complex. (4N)

ELGIN, Mark
The Public Relations Officer of Global Chemicals. (TTT)

ELITE
Literally chosen or set apart. The Doctor and his companions have encountered an elite element on Alzarius (5R), Skaro (4E), Varos (6V) and on Earth (4A) and also under its seas. (6L)

ELIXIR OF LIFE
The restorative liquid distilled from the Blue Flame on Karn. (4K)

ELIZABETH
The daughter of the squire in 17th century England whose manor house was taken over by the Terileptils. She was killed by them. (5X)

Eleanor of Wessex

ELIZABETH I
The British monarch at whose coronation the Doctor implies he was present, (MMM) and at whose pleasure he was detained (FFF). A conversation between her, Sir Francis Bacon and William Shakespeare was observed by the First Doctor and his companions on the Time-Space Visualiser given to the Doctor by the Xerons (R).

ELLUA
A princess from Earth who married the ruler of Peladon. She gave birth to the eventual king of Peladon and named him after her new world. (MMM)

ELYON
One of the Thal group encountered by the First Doctor on his original visit to Skaro. He accompanied Barbara, Ian, Antodus, Ganatus and Kristas on the rear offensive on the Dalek city. When filling the water bags for their journey, he was drowned by a mutant that lived in the pool. (B)

EMBODIMENT OF GRESS
A group of planets in the fifth galaxy which tried unsuccessfully to revolt against Zephon. (V)

EMBOLISM
The formation of an obstruction in a blood vessel. Mestor had the ability to cause this to happen by mental energy. He enslaved and even killed his subjects in this way. (6S)

EMERGENCY POWERS ACT
The Act which ordered the evacuation of London and left Charles Grover in charge of the city as the Minister with Special Powers. (WWW)

EMMETTS ELECTRONICS
The firm from whose factory Jeremiah Kettlewell's robot stole a focussing generator (4A)

EMPIRE STATE BUILDING
One of the locations in which the TARDIS materialised during the First Doctor's flight from the Daleks. (R)

THE EMPRESS
The interplanetary cruise ship, captained by Rigg, which was involved in a space collision with the *Hecate*. (5K)

ENDERHYTHE
The city where some women accused of being witches were subjected to a travesty of a trial, as mentioned by the Doctor. (7B)

ENGIN
The Coordinator at the time the Fourth Doctor was accused of assassinating the President of the High Council. (4P)

ENLIGHTENMENT
An Urbankan reduced by Monarch's technology to silicon chips, which were used to motivate an android body. (5W)

ENLIGHTENMENT
The prize in the Eternals' race. It was awarded to Turlough and appeared to be a huge diamond, but in reality was the rationality to make correct choices. (6H)

ENSEN GUNS
The weapons carried by Glitz and Dibber. (7A)

THE ENSIGN
A weekly boys' magazine for which the Master of the Land of Fiction wrote for twenty-five years up till 1926. (UU)

ENTROPY
A measure of unavailable energy, energy still existing but

lost for the purpose of doing work because it exists as the internal motion of molecules. It was through the release of entropy by the Master that Logopolis and the Traken Union ceased to exist. (5V)

ENZU
The Mogarian identity assumed by Hallet aboard the *Hyperion III*. (7C)

EOCENES
The more correct name for the Silurians, derived from the age during which the creatures flourished, as explained to Jo by the Doctor. (LLL)

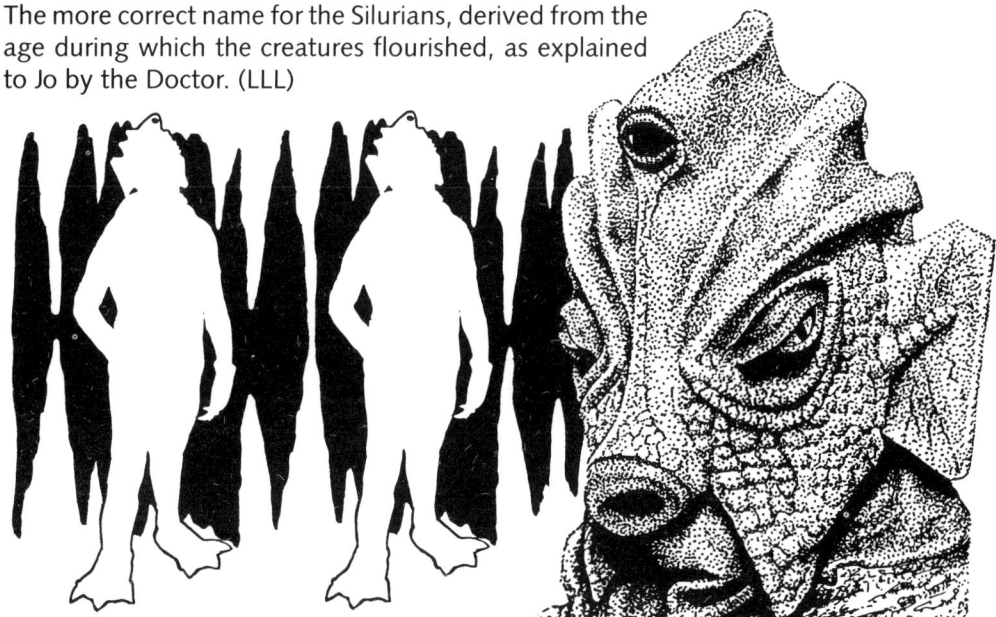

Eocenes

EPERJES-TOKAJ RANGE
A range of volcanic mountains, the eruption of which in 2030 was arranged by Salamander. (PP)

EPRIN
Altos' friend who was murdered in Millenius by Aydan, with which crime Ian was subsequently charged. (E)

EPSILON 4
The original destination of Rago and Toba's spacecraft before it made an emergency landing on Dulkis. (TT)

THE ERADICATOR
The weapon which Vorg used to destroy the Drashigs which escaped onto Inter Minor. (PPP)

ERAK
One of the crew of a scout ship from Gal Sec colony, stranded on Earth and forced to take part in Styre's experiments. (4B)

ERATO
The Ambassador from Tythonus to Chloris whom Adrasta had flung into the Pit. He was rescued by the Fourth Doctor. (5G)

Ergon

THE ERGON
A servant to Omega and one of his less successful attempts at psycho-synthesis. It was killed by Nyssa to stop its attack on the Fifth Doctor. (6E)

ERIC
The squire of Edward of Wessex. He was held captive and died in Irongron's dungeon. (UUU)

ERSKINE, Sergeant
A member of the Airport Police at Gatwick. (KK)

ESRITH
A Deon and inhabitant of Tigella. (5Q)

ESTO
A planet visited by Susan where the plants use thought transference for communication, as she related to Barbara. (G)

ESTRAM, Sir Gilles
The guise adopted by the Master when he attempted to pervert history at the time of Magna Carta. (6J)

ETERNALS
Beings which exist outside time and whose life span lasts forever. Their empty minds have the need for ideas which they extract from the brains of others whose minds they are able to read. (6H)

ETERNITY PERPETUAL COMPANY
The firm which manufactured the generators of the miniscope. (PPP)

ETHERIC BEAM LOCATOR
A device that can be used for detecting ion-charged emissions, which was in the Fourth Doctor's pocket when he was searched in the Bunker. (4E)

ETNIN
One of Cully's passengers, taken to the Island of Death on Dulkis. He was killed by the Quarks. (TT)

ETTA
An inhabitant of Varos and the wife of Arak. (6V)

ETTIS
A Peladonian miner who became so obsessed with ridding his planet of the Ice Warriors that he trained a booby-trapped sonic cannon on Queen Thalira's citadel and died in the ensuing explosion. (YYY)

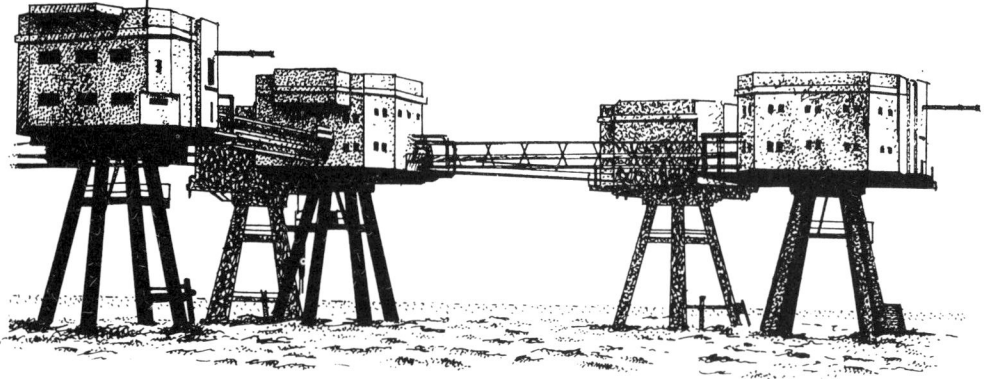

Euro-Gas Refinery

EURO-GAS CORPORATION
The company which owned the gas refinery in the North Sea where the Second Doctor fought the parasitic seaweed in 1972. (RR)

'EUSTACE'
The nickname given to the 12 million year old skull experimented upon by Doctor Fendelman. (4X)

EVANS, Doctor
The fourth member of the crew of the Moonbase. (HH)

EVANS, Driver
The cowardly Welsh driver of an ammunitions truck during the Yeti occupation of the London Underground. After being attacked by the creatures he became lost in the tube tunnels. (QQ)

EVANS, Dai
A miner at the Llanfairfach colliery and the second victim of *The Green Death*. (TTT)

THE EXAMINER
The official, sent for by Quinn to investigate the situation in the Vulcan colony in 2020, who was murdered by Bragen and impersonated by the Second Doctor. (EE)

EXO-SPACE
See E-Space

Jano, The Chief of The Elders and Exorse

EXORSE
A guard who served the Elders but became sympathetic to the plight of *The Savages*. (AA)

EXPERIENTIAL GRID
One of the choices for relaxation in the Leisure Hive which offered variable environments designed to stimulate physical, psychic and intellectual regeneration. (5N)

EXTINCT CIVILISATIONS
The book by Woris Bossard, which mentions the solar fireball which all but destroyed Ravolox, recalled by the Doctor. (7A)

Exxilon

EXXILON
The planet where the beacon atop its main city caused the TARDIS to lose power and the fire-power of the Daleks to fail. (XXX)

EYE OF HARMONY
The nucleus of a black hole and the inexhaustible energy source that powers all of Gallifrey (4P). It was drained of some of its energy by the Death Zone during Borusa's games (6K).

EYE OF HORUS
The power source of the force field which kept Sutekh paralysed in the Black Pyramid. It was destroyed by the Osiran through the agency of Marcus Scarman. (4G)

EYE OF ORION
The most tranquil place in the universe. It had a calming

effect on visitors because of the high bombardment of positive ions in its atmosphere. The Doctor took Tegan and Turlough there (6K) though he was unable to interest Peri in visiting it (6Y).

'EYE PLANTS'
The name given by Thals to a breed of flora on Spiridon which followed humanoid movements like an eye. They found them useful because they closed up when an invisible Spiridon was nearby. (SSS)

EYESEN
The court prosecutor at Ian's trial in Millenius and a conspirator in the case against him. (E)

Eckersley

F

Commander Fabian

FABIAN
The ground commander of the Interplanetary Pursuit Squadron. She sent Hugo Lang after the kidnapped Sylvest twins. (6S)

FALCHAN ROCKS
The region on Karfel which was the headquarters of the resistance group led by Sezon and Katz and where Peri was almost mutated with a morlox. (6Y)

FALSTAFF
The character in Shakespeare's plays based on the sixteenth century knight, Sir John Oldcastle. (R)

FANG ROCK
Part of a rocky island a few miles off the Channel coast taking its name from the jagged coastline there. A lighthouse was built on the island in the 1820s and soon after two men died there in mysterious circumstances while a third went mad with fear. This occurrence was attributed by legend to the 'Beast of Fang Rock'. It was thought to have struck again in the 1900s when the lighthouse crew and four passengers from a wrecked yacht were all killed in one night. In fact this latter incident was brought about by a Rutan. (4V)

FANTASY FACTORY
The headquarters of the Valeyard posing as J.J. Chambers and Popplewick in the Victorian England setting in the Matrix. (7C)

FARADAY, Colonel
The temporary commander of the British division of UNIT during the Kraal attempted invasion of Earth in the course of which an android duplicate of him was utilised by the aliens. (4J)

FARIAH
The woman forced into becoming Salamander's food-taster. She was shot by Benik's security guards. (PP)

FARLEY
One of the crew of the Edwardian sailing ship utilised by Striker in his race with his fellow Eternals. (6H)

FARRAH
A sweet manufacturing firm of Harrogate; in one of their empty toffee tins the Doctor kept a specimen of the Zeta Minoran minerals. (4H)

FARRAH
A swordsman in Prince Reynart's retinue. (5D)

THE FARRELL FAMILY
The owners of the plastics factory infiltrated by the Master to assist in the second Nestene attempted invasion of Earth. When the retired managing director, John Farrell, proposed having the Master removed from the factory the Master arranged for him to be killed by a plastic troll-like doll which was heat sensitive. His body was discovered by his wife, Mary. Their son Rex, a weak man, came under the Master's control and thus aided him in his alliance with the Nestenes. Rex was shot by Mike Yates when hypnotised by, and disguised as, the Master he assisted in the latter's escape. (EEE)

FARROW, Arnold
The ministry official killed by Forester in order that his anti-DN6 report should not be made public. (J)

FATIMA
The member of El Akir's harem who betrayed Barbara and Maimuna to the Saracen. (P)

FAY, Vivien
The identity which Cessair of Diplos assumed when she was pretending to work with Amelia Rumford. (5C)

THE FEDERATION
See Galactic Federation

FEDERATOR
The ruler of the Federation of Three Worlds, of which Manussa was a colony planet. (6D)

FEDERICO, Count
A tyrant and the uncle of Giuliano who coveted his nephew's dukedom of San Martino. He was burned to death by the Mandragora Helix working through Hieronymus. (4M)

FEDORIN
The Deputy Controller of the Central European Zone in 2030. He was poisoned by Salamander. (PP)

FELL, Ralph
The technical manager of Global Chemicals. He was controlled by the computer BOSS which drove him mad — to the point where he committed suicide. (TTT)

FENATIN
A member of the scientific elite on Skaro at the time of the creation of the Daleks, by whom he was killed. (4E)

FENDAHL
A creature from the legends of Gallifrey; something that had actually existed on the original fifth planet of the Solar System, before it broke up. Its skull managed to

travel to Earth where it eventually mutated Thea Ransome into a core for itself. It was a Gestalt – a group creature – composed of the core itself and twelve fendahleen. The Fourth Doctor contained the menace by using rock salt against the fendahleen and depositing the skull in a super-nova in the constellation of Canthares. (4X)

FENDELMAN, Doctor
The owner of Fendelman Electronics whose hobbies were archaeology and electronic research, the latter of which he pursued in his converted priory near Fetchborough. He was shot by Max Stael. (4X)

FENNER
The assistant controller of the protein refinery on Delta Three. (5E)

FERGUS, Alastair
The TV personality assigned to be the commentator on the opening of the Devil's Hump barrow for BBC-3. (JJJ)

Fedorin

FERRIER, Astrid
The personal assistant to Giles Kent. (PP)

FERRIGO, Luigi
The Genoan merchant who helped El Akir in the abduction of Barbara. (P)

FESTIVAL OF GHANA
The location of the exhibit the House of Horrors where the TARDIS materialised in 1996 during the First Doctor's flight from the Daleks. (R)

FETCH PRIORY
The building near Fetchborough which Doctor Fendelman had had converted into a home and a laboratory. (4X)

FETCHBOROUGH
The village where Ted Moss lived, near which stood Fetch Priory, owned by Doctor Fendelman. (4X)

FEWSHAM
The assistant controller of T-mat on the moon in the 22nd century. (XX)

ffINCH, Algernon
A lieutenant in the redcoat army barracked at Inverness in 1745. (FF)

FIBULI, Mister
The aide to, and friend of, the Captain. He was killed when the Mentiads 'threw a spanner into the works' as his commander was attempting to materialise Zanak while jammed by the TARDIS. (5B)

FIELD-INTERFACE STABILISER
The device which Scaroth blackmailed Romana into building for him, enabling him to go back to the time before his ship exploded. (5H)

FILER, Bill
The American Intelligence officer sent from Washington to liaise with UNIT over the capture of the Master. He also helped UNIT against the Master and Axos; during this incident he was duplicated by the space vampire. (GGG)

FINCH, General
The soldier given overall charge of military manoeuvres in London during its evacuation owing to the 'invasion' by dinosaurs. In fact he was one of the conspirators in 'Operation Golden Age'. (WWW)

FINDECKER
A 51st century scientist whose discovery of the double nexus particle sent the human science of that era into a technological cul-de-sac, as mentioned by the Doctor. (4S)

FISAR
A planet in the fifth galaxy which tried unsuccessfully to revolt against Zephon. (V)

FISH LANE
The street in London's East End in the 1890s where the Bullers lived with Nellie Gussett at number 14. (4S)

FISH PEOPLE
The farmers of Atlantis in the 1970s; humans with surgically added gills which permitted them to breathe under water. Polly was almost transformed into one. (GG)

FISHER, Kate
The singer at the *Last Chance Saloon* in Tombstone, Arizona in 1881. (Z)

FISK, Waterguard
An official from the Azure Customs and Excise Service

sent to investigate the collision between the *Empress* and the *Hecate*. (5K)

FISSION GUNS
Weapons from the armoury on Space Station Nerva used by Harry and Rogin against the Wirrn grub. (4C)

FITZROY SQUARE
The street where the TARDIS materialised in 1966 shortly after which the War Machines were mobilised by WOTAN. (BB)

THE FITZWILLIAM FAMILY
Sir Ranulf was a knight and the master of Wallingford Castle. He and his wife Isabella and son Hugh played host there to King John in March 1215, little realising that their monarch was in fact Kamelion and his champion, the Master, in disguise. (6J)

FLANNIGAN, Sean
The Irish Defence and Security operator aboard *The Wheel in Space*. (SS)

FLASH
The obnoxious customer at *The Inferno* who tried to make time with Polly until Ben rescued her from his attentions. (BB)

A Fish Person

Isabella Fitzwilliam And The Fifth Doctor

FLAST
The leader of the Cryons on Telos. She was killed by the Cybermen exposing her to heat. (6T)

FLAVIA
The Chancellor of the High Council at the time of Borusa's games in the Death Zone. (6K)

FLAVIUS GUISCARD
The owner of the villa in Assissium in which the First Doctor, Barbara, Ian and Vicki stayed. It is not clear whether he was known to the Doctor or not. (M)

FLAY FISH
A sea creature, native to Thoros Beta. (7B)

FLEET
The covered river in London which flowed under the Palace Theatre in the 1890s in which the giant rats,

created by the psionic amplification field of Magnus Greel's organic distillation plant, thrived. (4S)

FLEET STREET
The London road under which the Cybermen constructed their Earth base in 1986. (6T)

FLESH TIME
The name given by the Urbankans to the time of what they termed 'primitive, fleshly existence'; that is before they were reduced to silicon chips which were used to motivate android bodies. (5W)

FLETCHER
A UNIT corporal on duty in Tulloch when UNIT investigated the destruction of the oil rigs belonging to the Hibernian Oil Company. (4F)

FLEUR-DE-LYS
The public hostelry in the village of Devesham duplicated on Oseiden by the Kraals. (4J)

FLINT, Sir Percival
The employer of some Cornish miners who tried to open the Devil's Hump barrow in 1793. (JJJ)

FLORANA
A holiday planet, reputed to be the most beautiful in the galaxy, to where the Third Doctor was taking Sarah-Jane when the TARDIS was affected by the beacon atop the city of the Exxilons. (XXX)

FLORENCE
The Italian city visited at least once, in 1505, by the Doctor, where he implied that he had met Leonardo da Vinci on a previous occasion. (5H)

FLOWER
The young woman who acted as guide for Steven and

Dodo when they were shown around the city of the Elders. (AA)

FLUTTERWING
An insect native to Gallifrey, mentioned by Romana. (5B)

FLYNN, Johnny
A member of Reegan's band of thugs engaged to assist in the kidnapping of the alien ambassadors. (CCC)

Foamasi

FOAMASI
The reptilian race who fought against the Argolin. (5N)

FORBES, Corporal
A UNIT soldier whose patrol was on duty in Oxley Woods at the time of the Third Doctor's hospitalisation in Ashbridge. While driving a truck he spotted an Auton in its path. The truck crashed and he was killed. (AAA)

FOREMAN, I.M.
The owner of the junkyard where the TARDIS materialised in 1963. (A)

FORESTER
The unscrupulous owner of the firm which wished to market the insecticide DN6. (J)

FORGILL, Duke of
The Scottish nobleman who was impersonated by Broton. Honorary offices that he held included being Chieftain of the Antlers Association, Trustee of the Golden Haggis Lucky Dip and President of the Scottish Energy Commission. (4F)

FOSTER
One of Lieutenant Scott's troopers. He was killed by the Cybermen's androids. (6B)

FOSTER, Professor Howard
Peri's step-father, who was impersonated by Kamelion. (6Q)

FOSTERS
The main group of inhabitants on Traken, many of whom were simple gardeners. (5T)

FOX INN
The public hostelry in the village of Tulloch, of which Angus MacRanald was the landlord. (4F)

FRANKENSTEIN MONSTER
An android which the First Doctor encountered in the House of Horrors at the Festival of Ghana in 1996 during his flight from the Daleks. (R)

FRANZ
A German geologist and the thirteenth member of the crew of the Moonbase. (HH)

FRAX
The guard captain to the Mentors on Thoros Beta. (7B)

FRAZER, Colin
The cousin of Tegan whose will was dominated by Omega and thus forced to help his attempts to bond with the Fifth Doctor. (6E)

FREDDY
The stage doorman at the Palace Theatre in London's East End in the 1890s. (4S)

THE FREE
The primitive tribe on Ravolox, ruled by Katryca, which worshipped Haldron. (7A)

FRENCH REVOLUTION
The period in 18th century France which was the Doctor's favourite time in Earth history (H) and on which subject Barbara lent Susan a book (A) little dreaming that she along with her fellow teacher Ian, her pupil and the pupil's grandfather would soon visit that period (H).

FREREMONT, John
An official of the British Zone in 2030 murdered on the orders of Salamander. (PP)

Frankenstein Monster Android

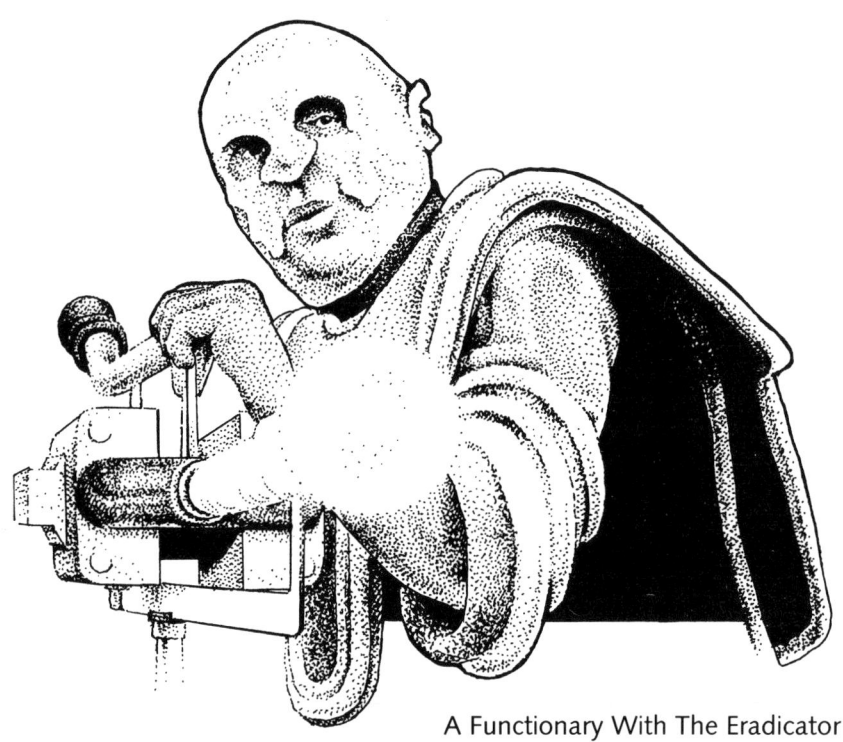

A Functionary With The Eradicator

FREYA
A domain on Tara of which Strella was the Mistress. (5D)

FRONTIOS
The planet on which the Tractators ensured that an Earth colony would be set up through their gravitational engineering forty years before the visit of the Fifth Doctor, Tegan and Turlough to that colony. (6N)

FROYN
A scientist at the Central City Experimental Block who conducted an experiment in molecular dissemination during which the First Doctor, Steven and Sara were transported to the planet Mira. (V)

FU PENG
The Chinese delegate to the World Peace Conference who replaced the murdered Cheng Teik. (FFF)

FULLER
An inmate at Stangmoor Prison. (FFF)

FUNCTIONARIES
The working class on the planet Inter Minor. (PPP)

FUNGOIDS
Plant life on the planet Mechanus. (R)

Fungoids

Queen Galleia

GAL SEC
The Earth colony from which Vural and his scouting party originated. (4B)

GALACTIC FEDERATION
An interplanetary alliance of worlds known more commonly as simply the Federation. Known members of the alliance were Alpha Centauri, Earth, Mars, Peladon and, at one time, Arcturus. A declared enemy of the Federation was Galaxy Five. (MMM, YYY)

GALACTIC SALVAGE AND INSURANCE
The London company formed in 2068 and liquidated in 2096, as an agent of which the Fourth Doctor posed when the TARDIS materialised aboard the interstellar cruise line the *Empress*. (5K)

GALATRON MINING CORPORATION
The company on Thoros Beta which employed Sil. (6V, 7B)

GALAXY FIVE
A conglomeration of worlds and the declared enemy of the Galactic Federation (MMM, YYY). By the year 4000 it was known as the Fifth Galaxy and was ruled from the planet Zephon (V).

GALAXY FOUR
The galaxy in which the planet Drahva was to be found. (T)

GALDRIUM
A mineral mined on Calufrax by the Captain. (5B)

GALLEIA
The wife of Dalios and the Queen of Atlantis at the time of the Master's attempted dominance of Kronos. (OOO)

GALLIFREY
The world in the constellation of Kasterborus from which the Doctor, Susan, Romana, the Master, the Rani and the Monk originate. It is also known as the Time Lord planet since that race is dominant among the others which inhabit it. These include the guards and other facile occupations who share the Capitol with the Time Lords and the Shobogans, mentioned by Spandrell (4P) and also the Outsiders who inhabit the wilderness beyond the Capitol (4Z).

GALLIPOLI
The battle during World War I which the Doctor mentions he has witnessed. (LLL)

GALLOWAY
A security officer in a military establishment in 2059. Kidnapped through time by the Daleks, he was shot by one of Lytton's mercenaries in 1984. (6P)

GALLOWAY, Doctor
The name which Edward Waterfield attributed to the Second Doctor when he sent Keith Perry to rendezvous with him in the *Tricolour* coffee bar. (LL)

GALLOWAY, Dan
A lieutenant in the MSC squad despatched to Exxilon for supplies of parrinium. In order to defeat the Daleks he hid aboard their saucer and blew it and himself up. (XXX)

GAME OF RASSILON
A series of tests devised by Rassilon in order to entrap any Time Lord seeking immortality. It was played by Borusa utilising the first five Doctors, Susan, Sarah-Jane, Romana, Tegan, Turlough and the Brigadier as pawns and resulted in his transformation into a living statue. (6K)

GAMMA MODE ENCRYPTION
The form of coding utilised on the Traken consular rings. (5T)

GANATUS
One of the Thal group encountered by the First Doctor on his original trip to Skaro. He accompanied Barbara, Ian, his brother Antodus, Kristas and Elyon on the rear offensive on the Dalek city. (B)

GANTRY, Kert
An agent of the Space Security Service who accompanied Bret Vyon on his mission to Kembel. He was killed by the Daleks. (V)

GANYMEDE BEACON
The space beacon to which a Pluto-Earth space flight dropover was diverted since Nerva Beacon was quarantined. (4D)

GAPTOOTH
A pirate on Samuel Pike's ship. (CC)

GARDEN OF FOND MEMORIES
A garden outside Tranquil Repose on Necros where relatives and friends of the dead mounted statues in their memory. (6Z)

GARDEN OF PEACE
A walled garden in the land of the Aztecs at the end of the 15th century, set out by Chapal, where all people over 52 years of age in their society could pass the remainder of their lives free from responsibility and care. (F)

GARDINER
The captain of the battleship which came to rescue cargo ship C-982 when it was looted by Ogrons. (QQQ)

GARGE
A criminal imprisoned on the planet Desperus, where he was eventually electrocuted. (V)

GARIF, Jaynis
A Decider on Alzarius at the time of the Fourth Doctor's visit there. (5R)

THE GARM
The huge, strong, wolf-like creature which was enslaved on Terminus by being subjected to a sub-sonic generator by Terminus Incorporated. He was released by the Fifth Doctor. (6G)

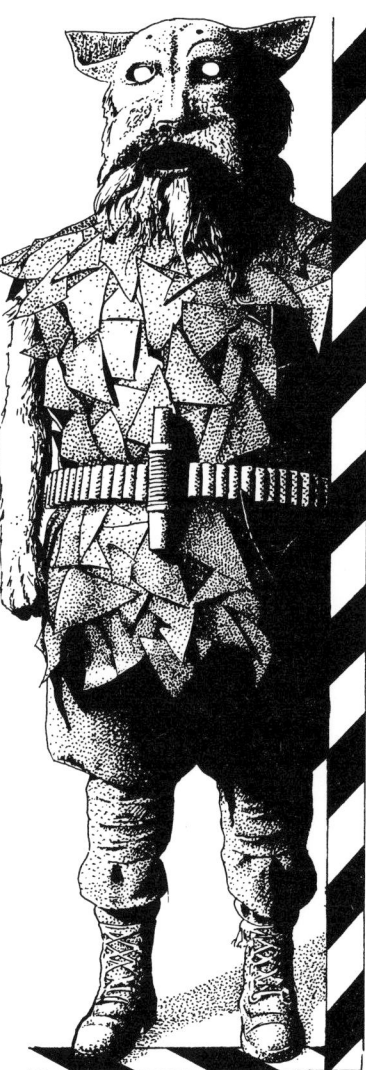

The Garm

GARRANT, Dal
A combat pilot serving in the Third Galactic Fleet of the planet Kantra. He was taken prisoner by the Daleks and forced to work for them on Skaro. He died there from exhaustion and malnutrition. (5J)

GARRET, Jan
The senior control technician at Britannicus base in 3000. (OO)

GARRON
A confidence trickster from Hackney Wick whom the Fourth Doctor encountered in the city of Shur on Ribos. (5A)

GARVEY, Jeff
A crewman on Lowery's space ship which brought Marc Cory to Kembel. On Kembel, he was pricked by a Vaaga plant and he gradually mutated into one of these plants. (T/A)

GARVIN
The verger of the church in the village of Devil's End. He was vaporised by Azal. (JJJ)

GASCOIGNE, Detective Inspector
The Scotland Yard detective enquiring into the disappearance of young people from Gatwick Airport. He was shot by the Chameleon utilising Spencer's body print. (KK)

GASTROPODS
Half-human and half-slug creatures from Jocondan mythology, to which race Mestor belonged. (6S)

THE GATEWAY
A way in and out of E-Space formed from the fabric of a CVE through which the TARDIS returned to N-Space. (5S)

 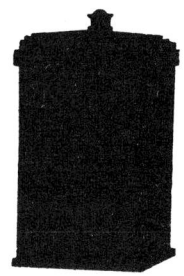

The Gateway

GATHERERS
Tax Officials on Pluto employed by the Company. (4W)

GATWICK
The London airport in which the TARDIS materialised in July 1966 where the Second Doctor discovered that the Chameleons were abducting young people and substituting themselves with their captives' body prints (KK). The TARDIS was stolen from there on the orders of Edward Waterfield under pressure from the Daleks (LL).

GAZAK
A rebel on the planet Karfel. He was thrown into the Timelash. (6Y)

GAZTAKS
A band of space mercenaries, originating from many planets, who were hired by Meglos and were led by General Grugger. They were destroyed when the Fourth Doctor inverted the control settings in Meglos' laboratory resulting in Zolfa-Thura and all on her being blown to bits, instead of Tigella which the mercenaries had intended. (5Q)

GEARON
One of the delegates to the Daleks when they formulated their Master Plan on Kembel. (T/A, V)

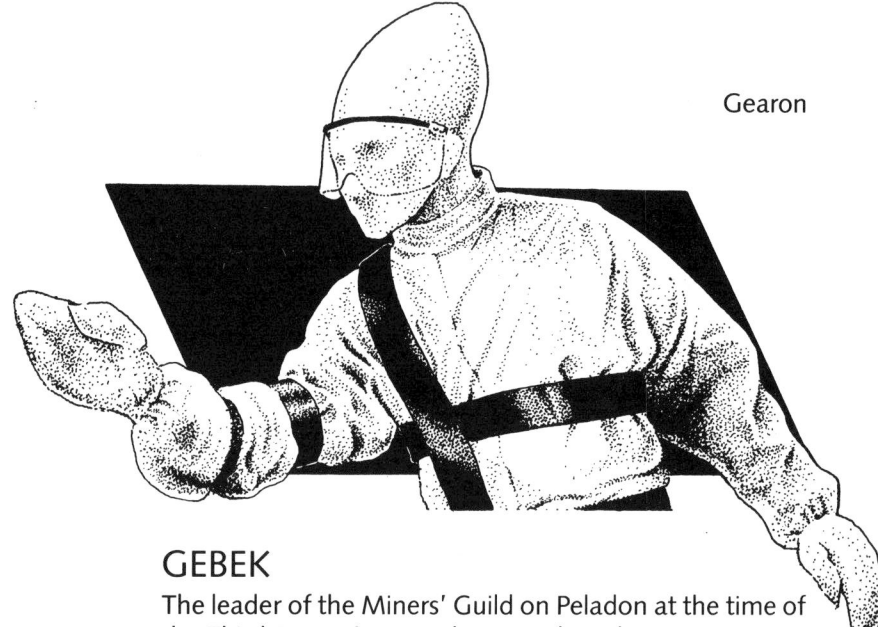

Gearon

GEBEK
The leader of the Miners' Guild on Peladon at the time of the Third Doctor's second visit to that planet. (YYY)

GEE-JEE FLY
An insect native to Varos. The Sixth Doctor was shown one, at which point he hallucinated that it had become greatly enlarged. This was caused by the effect of the purple zone of the planet on the visual cortex of the eyes. (6V)

Gell Guards

GELL GUARDS
Protoplasmic beings created by Omega. (RRR)

THE GENERATOR
The device in the Leisure Hive, more commonly referred to as the Recreation Generator, developed through the science of tachyonics by the Argolin for leisure pursuits. It produced Pangol who adapted it to clone himself to assemble a squadron to fight the Foamasi anew. He was defeated by the Fourth Doctor and reduced to a baby again by the introduction of Hardin's rejuvenation theories. These concerned tachyonics and were fed into the machine by Romana. (5N)

GENEVA
The Swiss capital city in which various organisations have their headquarters, viz. International Space Command (DD), the World Zones Organisation (PP) and UNIT (VV onwards) and to where the Brigadier had been called at the time of the Kraals' attempted invasion of Earth (4J) and also the crisis at Harrison Chase's residence (4L).

GENEVIEVE
The pseudonym under which Anne Chaplette passed herself when she briefly worked in the household of the Abbot of Amboise. (W)

GENTEK
The chief acolyte of the People of Tesh. (4Q)

'GEORGE'
The flippant name given to the android duplicate of Prince Reynart by the Fourth Doctor. (5D)

GERN
A Cyberleader who invaded the Geneva headquarters of International Space Command in 1986. He collapsed and died when Mondas exploded. (DD)

GERRILL
A Kaled soldier held prisoner with Sarah-Jane by the Thals. He was shot while attempting to escape. (4E)

THE GHANTA
A Tibetan bell from the Detsen Monastery given into the Doctor's safe keeping in 1630 and returned there by him in 1935. (NN)

GHARMAN
The Kaled head of the military elite on Skaro at the time of the creation of the Daleks, by which he was killed. (4E)

GIDI
A planet visited by Tryst's expedition. (5K)

GIOVANNI
A pikeman in the service of Count Federico in San Martino. (4M)

GIRTON, A/B
A sailor and one of the crew of the submarine sent by Captain Hart to investigate the sinking of ships in the English Channel. (LLL)

GIRTON, Tom
An inhabitant of the village of Devil's End who became a thrall of the Master. He made several attempts to kill the Third Doctor on the orders of the renegade Time Lord. During the course of one of them he was himself killed when the UNIT helicopter he had stolen crashed into the heat barrier created by Azal surrounding the village. (JJJ)

GIULIANO
The young Duke of San Martino whom the Fourth Doctor and Sarah-Jane helped against his uncle Federico, Hieronymus and the Mandragora Helix. (4M)

Giuliano

GLITTER GUNS
The weapons which, utilising the Cybermen's weakness against gold, were developed by their human adversaries turning the tide in the cyber wars and resulting in a resounding defeat for the metal beings. (4D)

GLITZ, Sabalom
A roguish space mercenary from the planet Salostophus with whom the Master allied himself in order to obtain the records of the violation of the Matrix by the Sleepers from Andromeda. He was sent by his employer to be a witness for the Sixth Doctor at the trial ordered by the High Council. (7A, 7C)

GLOBAL CHEMICALS
The company based in Llanfairfach whose computer, BOSS, planned to take over the world by linking up with every other major computer. (TTT)

GOBI DESERT
The arid region in Mongolia that Marco Polo's caravan crossed. (D)

GOLD
The precious metal which is deadly to Cybermen (4D, 6B) and which is to be found in abundance on Voga (4D). The seal of Kublai Khan worn by Marco Polo was made of gold (D). The bracelet which Barbara was given by Nero (M) was gold too as were the necklets with which the Animus controlled the Zarbi and a bracelet of Sarah-Jane's (UUU), and also a part of Adric's badge (6B). (N).

GOLD, Sir Keith
The Executive Director of Project Inferno. He had a counterpart on the parallel world visited by the Third Doctor, who died in a motoring accident. (CCC)

GOLD USHER
A ceremonial officer of the Time Lords (4P) and the official to whom was entrusted the investiture of Presidents. (4Z)

GOLF ALPHA CHARLIE
The call sign of the Speedbird Concorde, captained by Stapley, hijacked through time by the Master. (6C)

GOLF VICTOR FOXTROT
The call sign of the Speedbird Concorde, captained by Urquhart, hijacked through time by the Master. (6C)

GOMER
A Time Lord and Surgeon-General at the time of the attempted invasion of Gallifrey by the Vardans and the Sontarans. (4Z)

THE GONDS
A peace-loving race which became enslaved by the Krotons until the Second Doctor found a way to liberate them. (WW)

GOODGE STREET STATION
The London Underground station behind which Colonel Pemberton's patrol had its headquarters during the Yeti occupation of the tube system. (QQ)

GOODGE, Albert
A technician at the Deep Space Research Centre. He was shrunk and killed by the Master. (EEE)

GORSEDD
In Old Welsh literally a place of Augurs (people who can foretell the future); Boscombe Moor is one of the Three Gorsedds of the Isle of Britain along with Stonehenge and Bryn Gwyddon. (5C)

GORTON, Commandant
A conditioned British participant in *The War Games* in the World War I zone where he was the officer in charge of a military prison. (ZZ)

GOTAL
A subterranean dwelling Exxilon who aided the Third Doctor and Sarah-Jane against the Daleks. (XXX)

GOTH
The Chancellor of the Gallifreyan High Council who coveted the Presidency so highly that he agreed to help the Master in his quest for the Eye of Harmony. For his pains his ally killed him. (4P)

GOUDRY
A member of Mandrel's rebel band against the Company on Pluto. (4W)

THE GOVERNOR
The ruler of Varos whose decisions were judged by the people of the planet; failure in this political position there could easily lead to death by human cell disintegration for the post holder. (6V)

GRACHT
The estate on Tara of which Grendel was the master and where his castle was located. (5D)

THE GRAND ORDER OF OBERON
The fraternity to which Orcini belonged. (6Z)

GRANT
The news reporter who interviewed Mavic Chen before he set out for his first journey to Kembel. (V)

GRAPHOLOGY
The study of handwriting. Apparently it was a hobby of Victoria's since she chose to take a break from travelling with the Second Doctor and Jamie to pursue it while they visited Joinson Dastari on Space Station Camera. (6W)

The Governor of Varos

THE GRAVIS
The leader of the Tractators on Frontios. It was rendered harmless when the Fifth Doctor found a way to isolate it from the rest of its kind. (6N)

THE GRAVITRON
The device with which Jack Hobson and his staff controlled Earth's weather in 2070. It was based on the moon and was used by the Second Doctor to defeat the Cybermen there. (HH)

GRAVITY BEAM
The result of years of gravitational engineering by the Tractators; with it they were able to draw people through the ground, to bombard Frontios with meteorite fragments and even to draw Captain Revere's space ship there. (6N)

THE GREAT HEALER
The name behind which Davros hid while he experimented on Necros. (6Z)

THE GREAT INTELLIGENCE
A malignant disembodied entity, exiled from another dimension, condemned to hover eternally in space, forever craving form and substance. It possessed the power to take over humans' minds and make their bodies totally subservient to its will. It controlled the Yeti, robot servants who provided the strength needed in its plans of conquest. It was thwarted by the Second Doctor on two occasions – in Tibet in 1935 (NN) and forty years later in London (QQ).

THE GREAT JOURNEY OF LIFE
The manner in which the Nimon referred to their travels from planet to planet. Like a plague of locusts, they drained energy from each one. Their journey came to an end when the Fourth Doctor destroyed their complex on Skonnos along with three Nimon who had travelled there. This in turn set off a chain reaction which caused

Crinoth, where the remainder of the Nimon were located, to explode killing all on it. (5L)

THE GREAT ONE
One of the giant spiders on Metebelis Three who had reproduced her brain patterns with crystals in an attempt to increase her mental powers to infinity. When the Third Doctor placed the final crystal, the blue sapphire, in her web tremendous energy built up within her brain and destroyed her. (ZZZ)

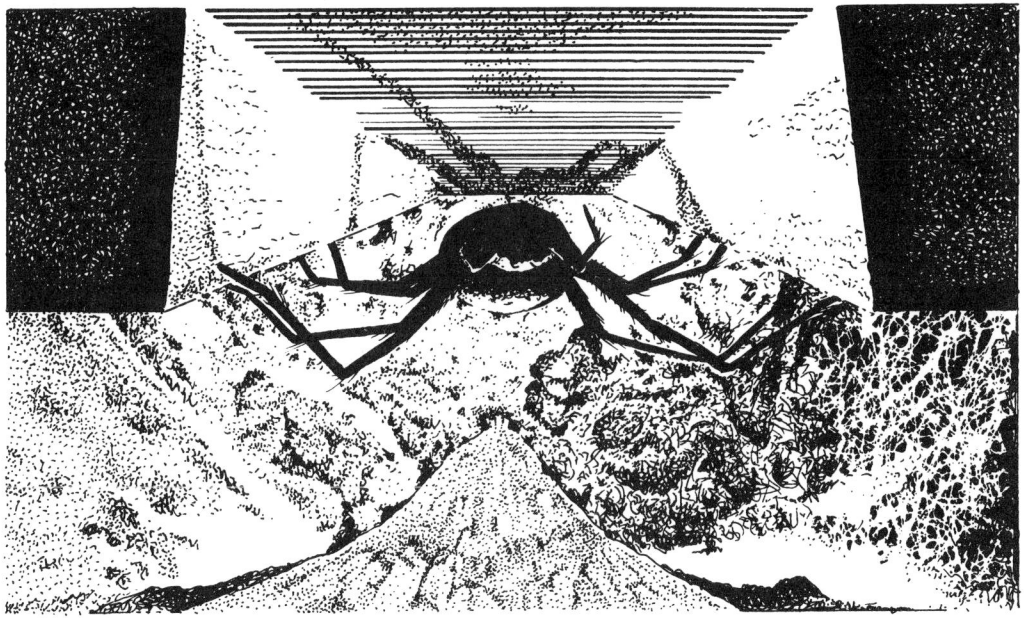

The Great One

THE GREAT VAMPIRE
The king of a giant race which fought against the Time Lords during the time of Rassilon. It fled into E-Space and settled on a planet there subsequently drawing the Earth space ship *Hydrax* there and forcing the crew to serve it by making them vampires too. It was destroyed when the Fourth Doctor auto-piloted an arrow-fronted scout ship from the *Hydrax* through its heart. (5P)

THE GREAT WEB
The name by which the Animus called its Carsenome. (N)

Magnus Greel as Weng-Chiang

GREEL, Magnus
A 51st century war criminal, nicknamed the 'Butcher of Brisbane', when he was Minister of Justice in the Supreme Alliance. He experimented with zygma beams and used them to flee through time to 19th century China. The experiment left him scarred and lacking in life essence. He was nursed by a peasant named Li H'sen Chang, who believed him to be the god Weng-Chiang, and the Peking Homunculus which he brought with him through time. While he was ill, the cabinet in which he had travelled was taken to England and he later set out to recover it. In order to keep alive he constructed an organic distillation plant which he used to extract the life essence from young women whom Chang procured for him. He was killed during a scuffle with the Fourth Doctor when he fell into his plant, accidentally activating it. He died of cellular collapse. (4S)

GREEN DEATH
An infection caused by contamination from waste products of Global Chemicals, so-termed because one of its symptoms was to turn its victims green. (TTT)

GREEN, Major
The head of security at the Post Office Tower in 1966, conditioned by WOTAN into serving its planned world conquest via *The War Machines*. (BB)

GREEN, Senior Prison Officer
One of Victor Camford's staff at Stangmoor Prison. (FFF)

GREEN, Edwin
A miner in Killingworth in the 17th century. He was operated on by the Rani and this turned him relentlessly aggressive. He was eventually killed by her. (6X)

GREEN, Steinberger P.
A Hollywood director whom the First Doctor encountered there briefly in the 1920s. (V)

GREGARIAN ROCK
The substance of which the statue aboard *The Ark* was sculpted. (X)

GREGORY
The Chief Researcher at International Electromatics. When UNIT freed Professor Watkins from I.E., Tobias Vaughn held him responsible and had him killed by the Cybermen. (VV)

GREGSON, Sir James
The Minister with Special Responsibility for T-Mat on 22nd century Earth. (XX)

GRELL
One of the guards who served Drathro. He was shot with a crossbow bolt by Merdeen. (7A)

GRENDEL
The Count of Gracht on Tara, a thorough villain who coveted his planet's throne. (5D)

GRENVILLE
An inhabitant of the village of Devil's End whose wife left him when he flirted with a younger woman. (JJJ)

GRENVILLE
The name under which Hallet boarded the *Hyperion III*. (7C)

GREY
A member of the Space Security Department who assisted Carrington in his plot against the alien ambassadors. (CCC)

GREY LADY
An android which the First Doctor encountered in the House of Horrors at the Festival of Ghana in 1996 during his flight from the Daleks. (R)

GREY, Solicitor
The prison commissioner who operated a trade in white slavery from Inverness with Jebb Trask in 1745. (FF)

GREYHOUND
One of the consistent call signs of UNIT. (JJJ onwards)

GRIERSON
The chief technician at the Space Defence Station outside Devesham. (4J)

The Grey Lady

GRIFFIN
A chef from the Australian district of Wooloomooloo, on the staff at Salamander's residence in the Central European Zone. (PP)

GRIFFITHS
A petty criminal whom Lytton engaged with a view to forcing him to help the Cryons. He was shot on Telos by a Cyberman. (6T)

GRIFFITHS, Doris
The cleaner at the Global Chemicals building in Llanfairfach. (TTT)

GRIGORY
A semi-alcoholic medic who helped Natasha Stengos to trace her father's remains. He was killed by a Dalek. (6Z)

GRIMWADE'S SYNDROME
The name by which robophobia is known among the Loyeed, as mentioned by the Doctor. (4R)

GROGAN
One of the crew of the Edwardian sailing ship utilised by Striker in his race with his fellow Eternals. (6H)

GROOM, Percy
The village constable of Devil's End. He was killed by Azal. (JJJ)

GROVER, Charles
The Minister with Special Powers placed in overall charge of London during its evacuation owing to the 'invasion' by dinosaurs. In fact he was one of the conspirators in 'Operation Golden Age'. (WWW)

GRUGGER
A self-appointed general and leader of the Gaztak band

General Grugger

employed by Meglos. He was killed when Zolfa-Thura exploded rather than Tigella since the Fourth Doctor had inverted the control settings in the Zolfa-Thuran's laboratory. (5Q)

GRUN
King Peladon's champion at the time of the Third Doctor's first visit to Peladon. (MMM)

GRUNDLE
The planet from one of the satellites of which the Drashigs originate. (PPP)

THE GUARDIAN
The last of a superior race on the planet Uxarieus who watched over the Doomsday Weapon. (HHH)

THE GUARDIAN
The minotaur who kept watch over the Crystal of Kronos in Atlantis. (OOO)

THE GUARDIAN OF DARKNESS
The more correct name of the Black Guardian; see that entry

THE GUARDIAN OF LIGHT
The more correct name of the White Guardian; see that entry

THE GUARDIAN OF THE SOLAR SYSTEM
The title used by Mavic Chen in the year 4000. (V)

THE GUARDIANS
The law-enforcement agents in the city of Millenius. (E)

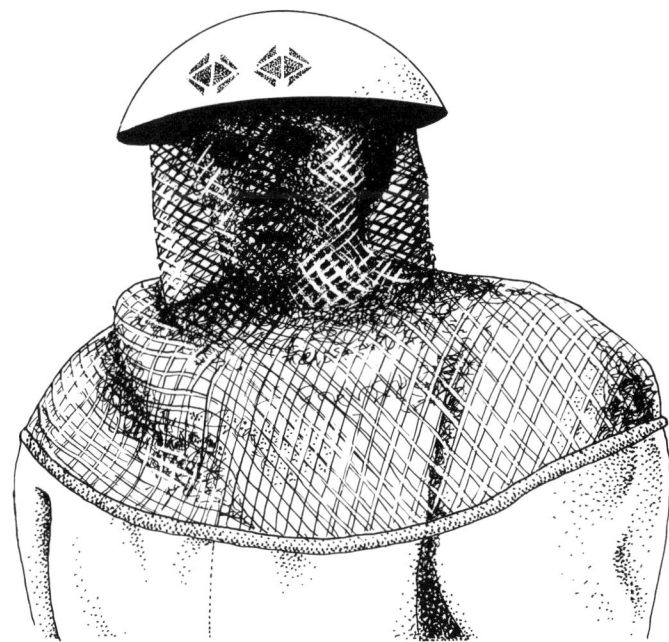
A Guardolier

THE GUARDIANS
The people travelling on *The Ark* to Refusis II charged with the care of the micro-reduced population from Earth. (X)

THE GUARDIANS
The armed troops of the Vogan guild. (4D)

THE GUARDIANS
Servicer-robots left on Mars by Horus to protect the power-source which kept Sutekh immobilised on Earth. (4G)

GUARDOLIERS
Guards which served the Maylin on Karfel. (6Y)

GUARDS
The middle level in the social structure on the planet which formed round the Minyan spaceship, the *P7E*, along with Trogs and Seers. (4Y)

GULLIVER, Lemuel
The fictional adventurer created by Jonathan Swift whom the Second Doctor encountered in the Land of Fiction. (UU)

GUM
The name given to the tribe of cavemen who sought to learn the secret of fire from the First Doctor. (A)

GUMBLEJACK
An alien water creature for which the Doctor has fished on several occasions, as he mentioned to Peri. (6W)

GUNDAN
Robots built by slaves on the planet in E-Space, where the Gateway to N-Space existed, for the purpose of killing their masters, the Tharils. (5S)

GUNNAR THE GIANT
A member of a Viking raiding party on England in 1066. (S)

GURN
A member of Sorenson's expedition to Zeta Minor who was destroyed by the anti-matter creature. (4H)

GURNEY, Zeb
The deceased chandler of the *Black Albatros*. (CC)

GUSSET, Nellie
The mother of Emma and mother-in-law of Joseph Buller, who lived at 14 Fish Lane in London's East End in the 1890s. (4S)

Hads In Action Against The Kroton

H.37
The classified explosive which killed Bruno Taltalian. (CCC)

HADS
Hostile Action Displacement System; a defence device fitted in the TARDIS. When operational it automatically dematerialises the space-time travel machine and moves it slightly in space and time. The Doctor has only been known to activate it once – on the planet of the Gonds. (WW)

HABRIS
The captain of the guard on the planet in E-Space where the *Hydrax* was drawn by the Great Vampire. He was strangled by Ivo. (5P)

HACKNEY WICK
The part of London from which Garron hailed. (5A)

HADE
A pompous, bullying Gatherer who worked for The Company on Pluto. When The Company employees revolted he was hurled to his death from a high building by the mob. (4W)

HAFSA
One of the women in El Akir's harem. (P)

HAINES
A technician at *Snowcap* base in 1986. He was killed by Krang. (DD)

HAJES
A deceased priest to Kroll about whom the Fourth Doctor read in the sacred book of the Swampies. (5E)

HAKIT
A B-grade technician who worked for The Company on Pluto. (4W)

HAKOL
A planet, for the inhabitants of which, tinclavic was mined by the Terileptils on Raaga. (6M)

HAL
An archer in the retinue of Edward of Wessex. He killed Linx by firing an arrow into his probic vent. (UUU)

HALDRON
The earth-god worshipped by the Tribe of the Free on Ravolox to whom they had erected a light converter as a totem pole. (7A)

HALERGAN III
The planet to which the Fourth Doctor proposed taking K-9 Mk. II, so they could spend a restful holiday. (5A)

HALL, Bob
The petty criminal with whom Kennedy worked in order to steal the TARDIS from Gatwick Airport in July 1966. (LL)

HALLET
An undercover agent on the *Hyperion III*, known to the Doctor. He took the guises of both Grenville and Enzu during his investigations and when dressed as the latter was poisoned by Doland. (7C)

HALLEY'S COMET
The comet, named for English astronomer Edmond Halley, with an elliptical orbit. In 1986, the Cybermen planned to divert its orbit so that it would crash into the Earth, thus preventing Mondas from being drawn into its twin's gravity field and eventually destroyed. (6T)

HAMILTON, Peter
A lieutenant in the MSC squad despatched to Exxilon for supplies of parrinium. (XXX)

HAMLET
The play by William Shakespeare. The inspiration for it came from Francis Bacon (R), and the Doctor copied out the first folio owing to Shakespeare's incapacity (5H). He also quoted from it while battling against the Valeyard (7C).

HAMPDEN, Jane
The village school mistress in Little Hodcombe. (6M)

HANNIBAL
The Greek general whom the Doctor implies he has met. (4A)

HARDIMAN, Sir George
The director of the Nuton Power complex. (GGG)

HARDIN
The particle engineer from Earth whom Mena brought to the Leisure Hive. Mena wished to employ his knowledge of tachyonics in its application to rejuvenation to assist the Argolin in developing the Generator. (5N)

HARDRADA, Harald
The king of the Vikings who raided England in 1066. (S)

HARDY
A crewman on the cargo ship C-982. (QQQ)

HARG
A technician at the protein refinery on Delta Three. He was killed when he was dragged into the swamp there by Kroll. (5E)

HARGREAVES
The manservant to Harrison Chase. He was choked to death by Chase's plants motivated by the second Krynoid. (4L)

HARKAWAY, Captain Jack
A fictional adventurer created for the periodical entitled *The Ensign* by the writer who became the Master of the Land of Fiction. (UU)

HARKER
The coxswain of the yacht on which Henry Palmerdale's party travelled from Deauville. He was killed by a Rutan. (4V)

HARKER, Captain
The regular army officer called in by Horatio Chinn to arrest the Brigadier and his UNIT group during the incident with Axos. (GGG)

HAROUN
The Arab merchant, full name Haroun ed Diin, who had vowed vengeance on El Akir for the deaths of his wife and son and the abduction of one of his daughters. He twice rescued Barbara from the Saracen and subsequently killed him to claim his revenge. (P)

HARP OF RASSILON
A musical instrument, reputed to have been played by Rassilon, kept in the council chamber of the High Council on Gallifrey. (6K)

HARPER
A partially conditioned North American participant in *The War Games* in the American Civil War zone. He was shot by the War Lord's guards. (ZZ)

HARPER, Seth
The gunman, nicknamed 'Snake-eyes', with whom the Clanton family allied in their quest for revenge on Doc Holliday in Tombstone, Arizona in 1881. He was shot by Holliday. (Z)

THE HARRIS FAMILY
Frank Harris was the Deputy Controller of the gas refinery in the North Sea owned by the Euro-Gas Corporation where the Second Doctor fought the parasitic seaweed in 1972. His wife Maggie was temporarily taken over by the intelligent weed. When Victoria elected to leave the Doctor and Jamie she stayed with the Harrises. (RR)

HARRY
The floor manager of the BBC-3 outside broadcast team assigned to cover the opening of the Devil's Hump barrow. (JJJ)

HARRY
Surgeon Lieutenant Harry Sullivan was the Medical Officer of UNIT. He had been seconded to UNIT from the Royal Navy. After public school Harry read medicine at Oxford where he also excelled in a variety of sports including cricket, rugger and boxing. Called upon to contend with the apparent collapse of UNIT's scientific adviser, Harry soon found himself involved as an undercover agent investigating members of the SRS on the

staff of Thinktank (4A). At the conclusion of this incident his remarks about the adviser's Police Box bridled the Doctor into taking him on a trip, during the course of which he encountered Wirrn parasites (4C), a Sontaran (4B), Daleks (4E) and Cybermen (4D) in quick succession before returning to present day Earth and a Zygon reception committee (4F). Following this he elected to remain on terra firma, declining the Fourth Doctor's offer of a lift back to London from Tulloch. However he was to help repel another attempted invasion of Earth, this time by the Kraals (4J), before he saw the last of the Time Lord.

The Fourth Doctor And Harry

While he was an excellent doctor and a model example in the skills of behaviour and discipline, Harry was possessed of a zealous enthusiasm which often led him to dive into situations without stopping to think. This occasionally landed him and/or his companions in hot water and for such a circumstance he was branded an imbecile by the Doctor (4D). His old-fashioned charm and protectiveness towards women, though well meant, was found by the liberated Sarah-Jane Smith to be both chauvinistic and sexist. During the course of his seven adventures with the Doctor he was impersonated twice by a Zygon (4F) and an android duplicate built by the Kraals (HJ) and only made one trip in the TARDIS; to and from the Ark in Space known as Nerva Beacon. After this time with UNIT his secondment was transferred to NATO, as the Brigadier related to the Fifth Doctor (6F).

HART, Sergeant
A UNIT soldier on duty at the time of the investigation of the caves on Wenley Moor. He was killed by the Silurians. (BBB)

HART, Captain John
The commanding officer of the naval shore base *HMS Seaspite*. (LLL)

HART, Teresa
An intended victim of Magnus Greel's organic distillation plant which extracted the life essence from beings, procured for him by Li H'sen Chang. Leela substituted herself for the woman enabling her to escape. (4S)

HARTMAN
An employee of Doctor Fendelman at his London premises of Fendelman Electronics. (4X)

HARVEY
A technician at the T-Mat base on the moon in the 22nd century. He was killed by the Ice Warriors. (XX)

HAWKINS, Captain
The Brigadier's deputy at the time of the UNIT investigation of the caves on Wenley Moor. He was killed by the Silurians. (BBB)

HAWKINS, Vince
An assistant keeper at Fang Rock lighthouse. He was killed by a Rutan. (4V)

HAWTHORNE, Olive
The inhabitant of the village of Devil's End who was a white witch. She aided the Third Doctor in his struggle to

prevent the Master from succeeding in obtaining Azal's power for himself. (JJJ)

HAYDON, Peter
An archaeologist among Eric Klieg's expedition to Telos. He was killed by the cyber-dummy in the target room above the tomb of the Cybermen. (MM)

HAYHOE LAUNDRIES LTD.
One of the guises for the van used by Reegan's thugs during their kidnapping of the alien ambassadors. (CCC)

HAYTER, Professor
The lecturer from the University of Darlington, specialising in hypnosis, who was absorbed into the Xeraphin life force. (6C)

THE HEARTS FAMILY
The King and the Queen and the Knave; opponents for Steven and Dodo in their enforced game of musical chairs in the realm of the Celestial Toymaker. (Y)

HEATHROW
The London airport where Tegan was to start work as an air stewardess. It was to Heathrow that the Fifth Doctor tried to return her (5W, 5X), finally succeeding in time to investigate the hijacking of two Speedbird Concordes through time (6C).

HECATE
The survey vessel, captained by Dymond, which was involved in a space collision with the *Empress*. (5K)

HECTOR
The Trojan prince, brother of Paris and Troilus, who while engaged in single combat with Achilles, the leader of the Myrmidons, was distracted by the TARDIS materialising. Thus his opponent gained the upper hand and slew him. (U)

HEDGES, Doctor

A medic at the Bi-Al Foundation whose will was taken over by the Nucleus of the Swarm. He was shot down by K-9. (4T)

HEDIN

A Time Lord and member of the High Council who blindly tried to assist Omega's attempts to re-enter the positive universe. He was shot by the current Castellan. (6E)

Hedin

HEETH
One of the crew of a scout ship from Gal Sec colony, stranded on Earth and forced to take part in Styre's experiments. He was killed by the Sontaran. (4B)

HEIRADI
The planet on which the Arar-Jecks lived, mentioned by Turlough. (6N)

HELDORF, Professor
A government scientist into whose care the alien ambassadors were placed. He was shot by Reegan's thugs. (CCC)

HELEN OF TROY
The Queen of Sparta whose abduction from her Greek husband, Menelaus, by Paris brought about the Siege of Troy. (U)

HELIUM
The gas which the Fourth Doctor had Leela use to distort Taren Capel's voice so that the robots aboard the sandminer would be unable to recognise it and therefore not obey him. (4R)

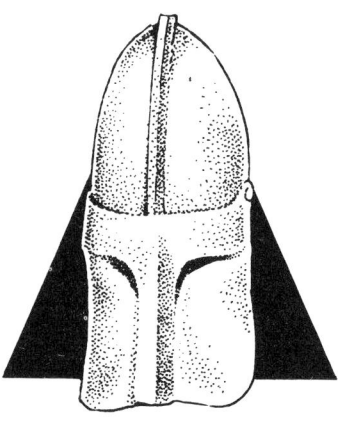

Helmet of Theron

HELIUM REGENERATOR UNIT
Part of the complex life-support system of beings from the planet Arcturus; its deactivation would cause their deaths. (MMM)

HELMET OF THERON
Theron was an Argolin who worshipped the flame of war. When he was killed in battle with the Foamasi his helmet became a sacred symbol to his people, but to Pangol it was a symbol of shame. A shame he felt forced to eradicate by wearing it himself in a new battle with the Foamasi. He cloned himself intending to lead a squadron of these clones into battle. (5N)

HELVIG, Lars
The Controller of the Scandinavian Zone in 2030. His 'suicide' was arranged by Salamander. (PP)

HENDERSON, Doctor
A doctor at Ashbridge Cottage Hospital. (AAA)

HENDERSON, Sergeant
A UNIT soldier detailed to assist the Doctor at Harrison Chase's mansion. He was killed by Chase. (4L)

HENRI OF NAVARRE
The protestant duke, married to the Princess Marguerite, the sister of Charles IX of France. The Huguenots would have liked to see him on the French throne. (W)

HENRY
A footman at Cranleigh Hall. (6A)

HENRY VIII
The British Monarch whom the Doctor mentions he has met. (G)

HENSELL
The governor of the Earth colony on Vulcan in 2020. He was killed by a Dalek. (EE)

HEPESH
The High Priest of Peladon at the time of the Third Doctor's first visit to that planet. He conspired with Arcturus to prevent Peladon's admittance to the Galactic Federation. His cruelty towards Aggedor was repaid when the royal beast killed him. (MMM)

HERCULES CLUSTER
A star grouping being monitored by Zoe when she first met Jamie on *The Wheel in Space*. (SS)

Hepesh

HERMACK, General Nicolai
The commander of the law enforcement organisation the International Space Corps. (YY)

HERMANN
The factotum to Count Scarlioni. (5H)

HERRICK
A member of Jackson's Minyan expedition which sought to find the space ship *P7E* that carried the Minyan race banks. (4Y)

HESLINGTON
An air traffic controller at Gatwick Airport in 1966 whose body print was taken over by a Chameleon. (KK)

HETRA
An Optera who helped the Menoptra and the First Doctor, Barbara, Ian and Vicki against the Animus on Vortis. (N)

HEXACHROMITE
A poison, deadly to reptilian life, which was used against the Sea Devils which invaded Sea Base Four in 2084. (6L)

HIBBERT, George
The managing director of Autoplastics who came under the domination of the Channing replica. He was killed by an Auton. (AAA)

HIBERNIAN OIL COMPANY LTD
The company whose rigs were attacked by the Skarasen. (4F)

HICKMAN, Edwin
One of only two crew on the oil rig that was one of the first targets of the Sea Devils. He was killed by a Sea Devil. (LLL)

HIERONYMUS
The astrologer to the court of San Martino who was secretly the leader of the Cult of Demnos in 15th century Italy. He was consumed by energy from the Mandragora Helix and his body simply collapsed when the Fourth Doctor managed to drain energy from it. (4M)

HIGH BRAINS
The term by which the Krotons referred to the super-intelligences of the Second Doctor and Zoe. (WW)

HIGH COUNCIL
The ruling body of the Time Lord civilisation, also referred to as the Supreme Council. It comprises a Chancellor (who is second-in-command), a Castellan, several Cardinals and Councillors, and, above all of these, the President. It is not to the credit of Time Lord society that several times members of that august body have been proven to be corrupt (4P, 4Z, 6E, 6K, 7C)

HIGH GALLIFREYAN
An ancient language of the Time Lords which fell into disuse. It is, however, understood by the Doctor. (6K)

HIGH MINISTER
A member of the World Executive at the time of the solar flares. Her recorded voice welcomed members of the Chosen to Space Station Nerva. (4C)

HIGH PRIEST(ESS)
The chief among leaders of worship. The Doctor and his companions have encountered High Priest(esse)s on Earth (F, 4M, 5C) and also Delta Three (5E), Exxilon (XXX), Karn (4K), Peladon (MMM, YYY), Tigella (5Q), Uxarieus (HHH) and in Atlantis (GG, OOO).

HILDA
One of the members of the Wholeweal Community based outside Llanfairfach. (TTT)

HILIO
The captain of the Menoptra spearhead invasion force to Vortis. (N)

HILL OF SORROWS
The site in San Martino where the TARDIS materialised in 15th century Italy. (4M)

HILLVIEW ROAD
The street in South Croydon where Sarah-Jane was living at the time of the Fourth Doctor's enforced abandonment of her. (4N)

HILRED
The commander of the Chancellery Guards at the time of Goth's treachery. He was shrunk and killed by the Master. (4P)

Hilio

HIMALAYAS
The mountain range at the foot of which the Detsen monastery was to be found and where the Great Intelligence concealed its spheres in 1935. (NN)

HINDLE
A member of Sanders' expedition to Deva Loka, he cracked under strain and then had his sanity restored by the Jhana Box. (5Y)

HINKS
The chauffeur to Justin Stevens. He was an unpleasant bully who was bitten by one of the giant maggots and thus infected with *The Green Death*. (TTT)

HIPPIAS
A young nobleman in Atlantis at the time of the Third Doctor's and Jo's visit there. He was slain by the Minotaur. (OOO)

HLYNIA
A Menoptra, enslaved by the Zarbi on Vortis, who rebelled against them with the help of Barbara and Hrostar. She then helped Hilio's spearhead invasion force and the time travellers to defeat the Animus. (N)

HO
A member of the Tong of the Black Scorpion. He was killed by Mr. Sin. (4S)

HOBSON, Jack
The irascible Yorkshireman who was the Director of the Moonbase in 2070. (HH)

HOLBORN STATION
The London Underground station where Driver Evans' ammunitions truck was ambushed by the Yeti during the

occupation of the tube system by the robots. (QQ)

HOLDEN, Jim
An electrician and colonist on Uxarieus. He was killed by the IMC spy Wilfred Norton. (HHH)

HOLLIDAY, Doctor John
The dentist who opened a surgery in Tombstone, Arizona in 1881 and involved the First Doctor in the Clanton family's quest for revenge. (Z)

HOPKINS
The boat-yard owner whose one-man hovercraft was utilised by the Third Doctor to chase Lupton. (ZZZ)

HOPKINS, Matthew
The 17th century witch hunter who terrorised witches near the village of Devil's End, as mentioned by Alastair Fergus. (JJJ)

HOPPER, Captain
The American officer in charge of the space orbiter in which Eric Klieg's expedition travelled to Telos. (MM)

Hobson

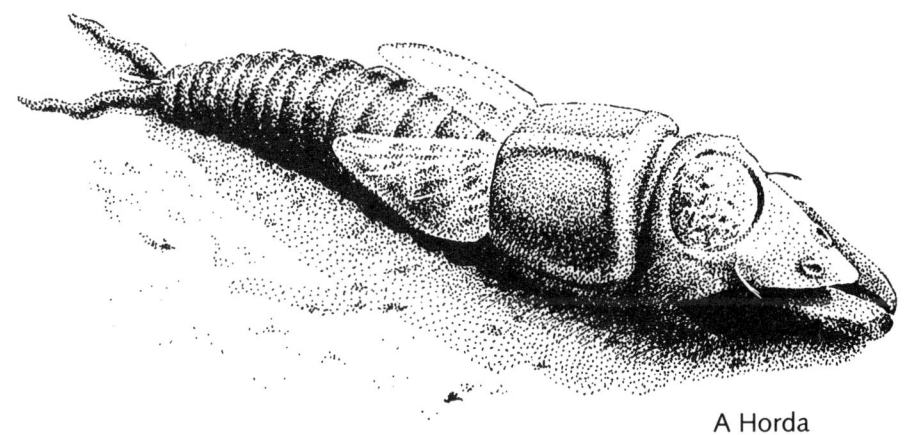
A Horda

HORDA
Carnivorous creatures on the world where Leela was born. (4Q)

HORG
The father of Hur and a member of the caveman tribe which tried to learn the secret of fire from the First Doctor. (A)

HORMUZ
The city where Marco Polo purchased his chess set. (D)

HORNER, Gilbert
The professor of archaeology whose excavation of the Devil's Hump barrow led to his being frozen to death when he released some of the power of Azal. (JJJ)

HORSE BOX
An outward shape taken by the Master's TARDIS. (EEE)

HORTON, Clive
An r/t operator in air traffic control at Heathrow airport. (6C)

HORUS
The Egyptian god of light who defeated his brother Sutekh by utilising a force field, and imprisoned him in the Black Pyramid. (4G)

HOUDINI, Harry
The Hungarian escapologist (real name: Ehrich Weiss) whom the Doctor mentions he has met. (ZZZ)

THE HOURLY PRESS
The tele-newspaper in 2000 in which the Karkus appeared as a cartoon strip character. (UU)

House of Horrors

HOUSE OF HORRORS
The exhibit at the Festival of Ghana in 1996 where the TARDIS materialised during the First Doctor's flight from the Daleks. (R)

HOUSE OF THE DRAGON
Magnus Greel's headquarters in London's East End in the 1890s. (4S)

HRHOONDA
A member of the Menoptra task force which Barbara encountered on Vortis. He was killed by the Zarbi. (N)

HROSTAR
A member of the Menoptra task force which Barbara encountered on Vortis. He was shot by a larvae gun. (N)

HUATH
The Queen Spider on Metebelis III. She was destroyed when Sarah-Jane broke the mental domination under which the Queen had placed her. (ZZZ)

HUCKLE
A company executive of the Hibernian Oil Company. (4F)

HUDSON, Mrs
The housekeeper to George Litefoot. (4S)

HUGHES, Ted
A miner at Llanfairfach colliery and the first victim of *The Green Death*. (TTT)

HULAGU
The Mongol warrior who had Ala-Eddin put to death, mentioned in Ping-Cho's recital to those travelling in Marco Polo's caravan. (D)

THE HUMAN FACTOR
The essence of the make-up of human beings which is unique to them. In order to determine it the Daleks arranged for Jamie to rescue Victoria Waterfield whom they held captive. Once they had diagnosed the factor they utilised it to increase their own 'Dalek Factor' so that they would become invincible against humans. (LL)

HUMKER
An inhabitant of Ravolox who passed Drathro's selection test and was therefore permitted to serve it. (7A)

THE HUNTSMAN
A native of the planet Chloris. He acceded to the temporary rule of the planet after his mistress, the Lady Adrasta, was killed by Erato. (5G)

HUR
The daughter of Horg and a member of the caveman tribe which tried to learn the secret of fire from the First Doctor. (A)

HUTCHINSON, Sir George
The local magistrate in Little Hodcombe who came under the influence of the Malus, which eventually consumed him. (6M)

HUXLEY, Aldous
The English novelist and essayist whom the Doctor implies he has met. (5V)

HYDE, Stuart
A post-graduate student at the Newton Institute who worked unknowingly for the Master. (OOO)

THE HYDRAX
An Earth exploration vessel which when bound for Beta Two vanished into E-Space drawn to a planet there by the Great Vampire. The crew, Captain Miles Sharkey, Navigation Officer Lauren Macmillan and Science Officer Anthony O'Connor were turned into vampires. They settled on the planet, living in the *Hydrax* which became their palace, adopting the names of Zargo, Camilla and Aukon. (5P)

HYDRAZINE STEAM GENERATOR
A defunct machine which had once provided interior lighting for the colonists on Frontios. (6N)

HYDROMEL
The symptom-suppressing drug against Lazar Disease supplied to the Vanir by Terminus Incorporated. (6G)

HYKSOS
A guard captain in ancient Egypt. He was killed by the Daleks. (U)

HYMETUSITE
A radioactive mineral, supplies of which young Anethans were forced to bring to the Nimon on Skonnos, where it was used to power an energy beam. (5L)

HYPERION
The space ship in which the Earth Council investigator travelled to Solos. (NNN)

HYPERION III
The space cruiser, captained by Commodore Travers. Flight 113 was disrupted in 2986 by the ambitions of Rudge, its security officer, the plans of the Mogarians, the schemes of Doland and terror by the Vervoids. (7C)

HYPERON
The planet from which a rocket fleet devastated the Daleks in the space year seventeen thousand, as mentioned by the Doctor. (4E)

I

Interplanetary Mining Corporation

ICCA
The Inner Constellations Corrective Authority; the body to which Pletrac proposed to hand over the Third Doctor to investigate his status as an illegal alien on Inter Minor. (PPP)

IDBI
I Don't Believe It; uttered by Steven after Vicki had explained to him about the TARDIS. (S)

IE
International Electromatics; the company of which Tobias Vaughn was the managing director. (VV)

IF
Index File; part of the data base of the TARDIS' computerised information system. (5Z)

ILF
Intelligent Life Form; as used by Sanders' expedition to Deva Loka. (5Y)

IMC
Interplanetary Mining Corporation – the company whose squad on Uxarieus under Captain Dent terrorised the colonists there in order that they could mine exclusively for duralinium on the planet. (HHH)

IRIS
Image Reproduction Integrating System; a machine developed by the Doctor which translates thoughts into pictures on a screen. (ZZZ)

ISC
International Space Command; the defence organisation with a headquarters in Geneva and a rocket base, named *Snowcap*, in the Antarctic. (DD)

IAN
Abducted from his own world and time, Ian Chesterton was at first angry at, and subsequently resigned to, the situation into which he and Barbara Wright had thrust themselves when he and his fellow teacher from Coal Hill School had taken an interest in a strange pupil known to them as Susan Foreman.

Once he and Barbara understood the Doctor's reason for taking them with him and his frustration at subsequently being unable to return them to London in 1963, he adjusted to the situation and assumed the role of champion and defender of the group of wanderers in space and time.

Ian taught science, but thrust into the environment of the paleolithic age he found that his university education was of little use to him and was forced to fall back on his physical strength and personal courage (A). A desperate situation required a desperate solution. Accepting his fate, he then relaxed and resumed being the patient man with a sense of humour that he had been as a school teacher.

Since he was visibly the strongest of the four travellers, whether the fourth was Susan or Vicki, Ian was often taken to be the leader among the group and because he was young and strong he often had to be the one to take risks to protect his friends. It was Ian who convinced the Thal group on Skaro that they should fight the Daleks (B); it was Ian who formed a relationship of mutual respect with Marco Polo (D); it was Ian who was chosen as a leader in their army by the Aztecs (F) and it was his courage and chivalry which were rewarded by Richard the Lionheart with a knighthood (P). Throughout his adventures with the Doctor, Ian remained almost unaffected. Perhaps richer in knowledge for his experiences, when he left he was still the outwardly easy-going young man, a little short tempered, with the humorous, modest outlook that he had had when he first entered the TARDIS in Totters Yard.

Ian

Although outwardly easy-going no one rode roughshod across Ian Chesterton in whatever circumstances he found himself. He was an ordinary and remarkable young man, a pawn of a fate, that was at first beyond his comprehension, but which forced him to become heroic. This heroic quality allowed him always to win through in the end.

He grew weary of his fate, but was powerless to attempt to alter it until the deserted Dalek timeship on Mechanus presented both Barbara and himself with one slim chance to return to the world they knew. Together they accepted the challenge and Ian returned to 20th century London like a hero home from the wars. His first new challenge being to explain why he and Barbara had been missing for two years (R). No doubt he also coped with that dilemma admirably!

IBBOTSON, 'Hippo'
A pupil at Brendon School whom Turlough befriended. (6F)

IBRAHIM
An Arab bandit who held Ian prisoner in the desert and then helped him to rescue Barbara from El Akir. (P)

ICE SOLDIERS
The custodians of one of the micro-circuit keys of the Conscience of Marinus. (E)

ICE WARRIORS
A reptilian militaristic race from Mars, the red planet. They recognise no morality in conflict, despising the weak and respecting only superior force. They are ready to eliminate callously any being who is of no use to them as the scavenger Storr discovered when he failed to make an alliance with them in 3000 (OO). They are a proud race, indeed almost arrogant in their own ability to resolve any given situation in their favour as witness Izlyr's reactions on Peladon when the Doctor's mistrust of them led him to suspect them of collusion with Galaxy Five (MMM). Nobility too is one of their characteristics which Izlyr's reactions clearly illustrate, as indeed do Slaar's and Azaxyr's actions on the moon (XX) and Peladon (YYY) respectively, although the Doctor would not agree with them.

There are at least three ranks in the strata of the Ice Warriors' strictly ordered hierarchy: the rank and file soldier and non-commissioned officers—Varga (OO) and Ssorg (MMM), the Ice Lords—Slaar (XX), Izlyr (MMM) and Azaxyr (YYY) who act as field commanders, and the Marshal (XX), clearly a leader in their civilisation.

Ice Warriors cannot exist in the atmosphere of Earth and Peladon without the higher oxygen content of both these planets affecting their voices so that they have a rasping quality to them. However when aboard a Martian space vessel the Grand Marshal had no such speech difficulty.

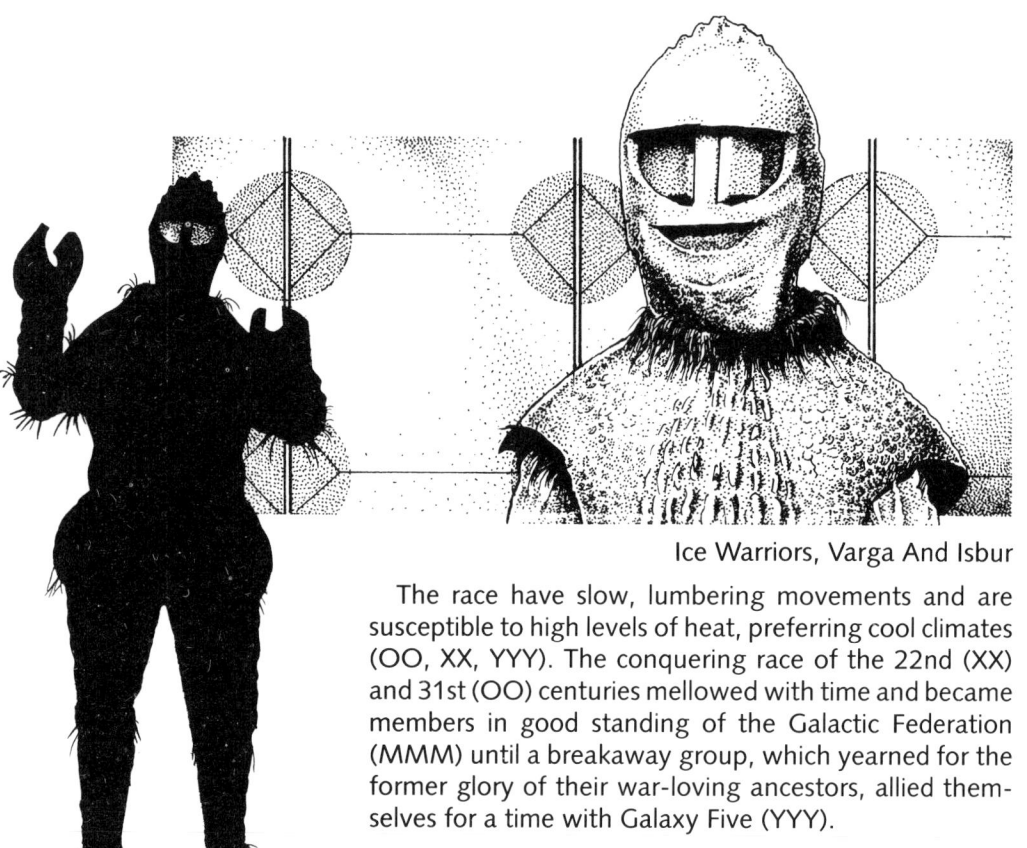

Ice Warriors, Varga And Isbur

The race have slow, lumbering movements and are susceptible to high levels of heat, preferring cool climates (OO, XX, YYY). The conquering race of the 22nd (XX) and 31st (OO) centuries mellowed with time and became members in good standing of the Galactic Federation (MMM) until a breakaway group, which yearned for the former glory of their war-loving ancestors, allied themselves for a time with Galaxy Five (YYY).

ICTHAR
The leader of the Silurian Triad which attacked Sea Base Four in 2084. He was shot by Turlough. (6L)

IDAS
A Trog, son of Idmon, on the planet which formed round the Minyan space ship, the *P7E*. (4Y)

IDMON
A Trog, father of Idas, on the planet which formed round the Minyan space ship, the *P7E*. (4Y)

IMAGE REPRODUCTION INTEGRATING SYSTEM
See IRIS

INFERNO
The night club where Ben and Polly first met one another. (BB)

INGA
A lazar on Terminus who befriended Nyssa. (6G)

THE INGLENOOK
The inn in 17th century Cornwall, of which Jacob Kewper was the landlord. (CC)

INGRAM, Ruth
The research assistant assigned to work for Professor Thascalos at the Newton Institute. (OOO)

INNER CONSTELLATIONS CORRECTIVE AUTHORITY
See ICCA

INOKSHI
The solar system in which Urbanka was to be found. (5W)

THE INQUISITOR
A Time Lady appointed to preside over the trial of the Sixth Doctor by the High Council. She was one of the Gallifreyans the Council had secretly commissioned the Valeyard to kill. (7A/B/C)

INTELLIGENT LIFE FORM
See ILF

INTER MINOR
The planet where the Third Doctor and Jo were trapped inside the miniscope belonging to Vorg. (PPP)

INTERNATIONAL SPACE CORPS
The law enforcement organisation in which Hermack and Warne were officers. (YY)

INTERPLANETARY MINING CORPORATION
See IMC

INTERPLANETARY PURSUIT SQUADRON
The law enforcement agents at the time of the abduction of the Sylvest twins. (6S)

INVERNESS
The city where Algernon ffinch was barracked in 1745 and from where Solicitor Grey operated a trade in white slavery. (FF)

ION
An electrically charged particle formed by the loss or gain by an atom of electrons, effecting by its migration the transport of electricity. Nyssa found a way to utilise ions to make a weapon (5T) while on Earth in 3000 they were used for basic power (OO) as they were in the recreation rooms in the Leisure Hive (5N) and to propel the Eternals' ships (6H). The Eye of Orion had a calming effect on visitors to it because of the high bombardment of positive ions in its atmosphere (6K).

ION BONDER
A device perfected by Nyssa which she used as a stun weapon. (5T, 5Z)

IONIC COLUMN
The outward shape taken by the Master's TARDIS on several occasions. (5V, 5Z, 6C)

IONISER
The machine maintained at Brittanicus base in 3000, the

purpose of which was to combat the threat of another Ice Age on Earth by intensifying the sun's heat. The Second Doctor found a way for Penley to use it as a weapon against Varga's patrol of Ice Warriors. (OO)

IRONGRON
The medieval captain who usurped Edward of Wessex and initially cooperated with Linx, who eventually killed him. (UUU)

ISBUR
One of Varga's patrol of Ice Warriors found frozen near Brittanicus base in 3000. He was destroyed along with his colleagues when Penley blasted their ship into oblivion using the Ioniser. (OO)

ISLAND OF DEATH
A poisonous wasteland on Dulkis which resulted from its having been used as a centre for atomic energy tests. It was preserved as a warning to future generations together with an anti-war museum set up there. It was there that the Dominators' space craft made its emergency landing and there that the TARDIS materialised on the Doctor's second visit to Dulkis. (TT)

ISOP GALAXY
The galaxy in which Vortis is to be found. (N)

ISSIGRI FAMILY
The family which ran the Issigri Mining Company which mined for argonite on the planet Ta. Madeleine at first cooperated with the space pirate Maurice Caven but deserted him when she learned that Caven had kidnapped and kept prisoner her father, Dom, whom she thought dead. (YY)

THE ITHACONS
The Greek troops led by Odysseus. (U)

IVO

The headman of the village on the planet in E-Space where the *Hydrax* was drawn by the Great Vampire. (5P)

IXTA

The son of Chapal and a chosen warrior among the Aztecs at the end of the 15th century. He fell over a parapet to his death during an attack he made on Ian. (F)

IZLYR

An Ice Lord and the Martian delegate to the Galactic Federation at the time that the alliance was considering the planet Peladon's suitability for Federation membership. (MMM)

Izlyr

J

Jackson (4Y)

JA 566
The registration number of the Brigadier's vintage Humber car, wrecked when Turlough crashed it. (6F)

JABEL
The Captain of the People of Tesh. (4Q)

JACK
One of the MSC squad despatched to Exxilon for supplies of parrinium. He was killed by natives of that planet. (XXX)

JACKIJ
The Professor on Androzani Minor who discovered the cure for spectrox toxaemia. (6R)

JACKO
A ship-wrecked West Indian rescued by the Atlanteans and then forced to work in their mines. With the help of the Second Doctor, Ben, Polly and Jamie he was able to regain his freedom. (GG)

JACKSON
The leader of the Minyan quest to find the space ship *P7E* which carried the Minyan race banks. (4Y)

JACKSON
The helmsman of the Edwardian sailing ship utilised by Striker in his race with his fellow Eternals. (6H)

JACKSON, Miss
The personal assistant to Owen Watson, the Director of the Nunton Experimental Complex. (4N)

JACKSON, Private
A UNIT soldier on duty in Tulloch during the investigation of the attacks on the rigs belonging to the Hibernian Oil Company. (4F)

JAEGER
An Earth scientist who worked in Skybase above Solos in the 30th century under the Marshal. He was killed when particle-reversal apparatus exploded. (NNN)

JAGAROTH
A vicious, callous, war-like race. The last survivor, Scaroth, was slivered throughout time and plotted unsuccessfully to change Earth's pre-history in order that his people might survive. (5H)

JAGO, Henry Gordon
The manager of the Palace Theatre in London's East End in the 1890s. (4S)

THE JAILER
The keeper of the Conciergerie prison during *The Reign of Terror*. (H)

JALL
A passenger on a space shuttle raided by the Daleks. He was among those aboard taken prisoner, brought to Skaro and forced to work for their captors. (5J)

JAMAICA
A pirate on Samuel Pike's ship. He was killed by his captain. (CC)

JAMES
An employee of Global Chemicals; Mike Yates freed him from control by the BOSS through the use of the Metebelis crystal. He was still linked to the computer and it immediately killed him. (TTT)

JAMES
A footman at Cranleigh Hall. He was strangled by George Cranleigh. (6A)

JAMIE
James Robert McCrimmon was born into the clan known for providing Scotland with its finest pipers. He grew up to become one of the brave Highland Pipers who marched at the front of the Young Pretender's army when it faced the English cannons at the Battle of Culloden in 1745. Jamie survived the slaughter on that day and limped away with Colin, the Laird of the McLarens, and his family. Their paths crossed with that of the Second Doctor, Ben and Polly and after Jamie had helped the three time travellers to thwart the plans of the corrupt Solicitor Grey he guided them back to the TARDIS. Since the Redcoat soldiers were still very much in evidence Polly suggested taking him with them and after a pause for thought the Doctor agreed and thus Jamie's travels began (FF).

It was probably fortuitous for the young Scot that the Doctor had regenerated his old first body into the rejuvenated form whose eccentricities Jamie would come to prize very highly. In this new body the Doctor lost many of the tendencies towards tetchiness and impatience, which he had exhibited previously towards those who were unable to grasp what were for him, basic scientific principles. Jamie's knowledge was somewhat limited because of the age which had spawned him and it fell to the Doctor, Ben, Polly and, later, Zoe to explain everyday basics to him.

After only one foray away from his native Scotland, Jamie was easily goaded by Ben into teasing the Doctor about his ability to control the TARDIS. The result being that a planned trip to Mars terminated on the Moon (HH). This Jamie was unable to accept because the Moon is up in the sky!

Ben and Polly elected to remain in 1966 after the defeat of the Chameleons but Jamie was destined to rescue Victoria Waterfield and to become quite fond of her during her time with the Doctor. He was still no match for her intellectually. Coming from 120 years later than he did, Victoria was able to explain about the Yeti to him (NN). However, he hovered around her person devotedly and protectively and his relationship with her became one of brother-sister. It is perhaps not very surprising that, since both were orphaned and cut off from their own time, they gravitated towards one another and each seemed to enjoy the other's company. However, while Jamie relished his adventurous time-hopping lifestyle, Victoria was looking ultimately for security. She opted to find this with Frank and Maggie Harris (RR). After that even the Doctor's jollity could not lift Jamie's depression (SS).

His introduction to Zoe Herriot was not very auspicious and their relationship was never as close as his with Victoria. Zoe was not just bright, she was a prodigy and trainee genius and whereas Victoria was more than happy to let Jamie perform the heroics Zoe more often than not seemed prepared to take risks herself. In her company Jamie was virtually eclipsed by the brilliance of the diminutive astrophysicist, though he did steal a march on her when he was able to explain 'primitive' candles to her (YY).

Basic practicality was one of Jamie's fortes; he accepted space ships as there seemed no point in not accepting their existence. If he was able to provide himself with an explanation for futuristic science, such as equating T-Mat with a flying carpet (XX), so much the better.

His valour, bravery and courage came to be unquestionable, particularly so when, against the Doctor's advice, Jamie rescued Victoria when she was being held captive by the Daleks (LL). He did sometimes accept unnecessary challenges too easily, like that from Axus (WW). His leaps into the fray were often accompanied by the rally cry of "Creag an Tuire".

He suffered a unique fate among the Doctor's companions when he temporarily lost his original face in the fantasy world of the Land of Fiction (UU). He was one of the companions who crossed paths with more than one of the Doctor's regenerations (6W), a fact he also just had to accept.

Jamie And The Second Doctor

When the Time Lords returned him to his own time his memories of his adventures with the Doctor after the events in 1745 were erased by them. They did not stop the Doctor himself from remembering though, a fact which helped him to defeat Borusa when Jamie's ghost was summoned up by the Lord President in the Death Zone (6K).

JAMIESON BOYS
Two brothers, Donald and Robert, who had a terrifying experience on Tulloch Moor in 1870 – the former disappeared and the latter was driven mad by it – as related to Sarah-Jane by Angus MacRanald. (4F)

JANET
A stewardess on the *Hyperion III*. (7C)

JANIS THORN
Part of a plant on the world on which Leela was born. Being pricked by one produced instant paralysis followed by almost inevitable death. Leela used one on a Sevateem guard (4Q) and another on a member of the Tong of the Black Scorpion who threatened the Fourth Doctor. (4S)

JANLEY
The assistant to Lesterson in the Earth colony on Vulcan in 2020. She was a member of Bragen's group of rebels and was exterminated by the Daleks. (EE)

JANO
The Chief Elder on the planet of *The Savages*. (AA)

JANOS
A member of Salamander's security forces. (PP)

JARL
One of Krang's cyber patrol which invaded *Snowcap* base in 1986. He was shot down by Ben. (DD)

JASKO
One of the Gallifreyans inhabiting the wilderness beyond the Capitol on the Time Lord planet. He was killed in a skirmish with Sontaran troupers. (4Z)

JASONITE
A black crystal substance found on Crinoth which Sezom discovered acted as a powerful electro-magnetic booster to the power of the staff of office given to him by the Nimon. He was able to turn that power against them. (5L)

JEAN
A bourgeois friend of Jules Renan who opposed the rule of Robespierre during *The Reign of Terror*. (H)

JEAN-PIERRE
The boy who helped the First Doctor escape from a burning building during *The Reign of Terror*. (H)

JEK, Sharaz
A scientist from Androzani Major who worked in the spectrox industry. His partner Trau Morgus arranged an 'accident' which was planned to kill him leaving Morgus in sole control of that industry. He was caught in a scalding mud burst; however it did not kill him as intended, but left his face dreadfully scarred. After that, he wore a mask in order not to be shunned by others. He fled to Androzani Minor where he perfected his field of knowledge – the construction of androids – and planned for his hour of revenge on Morgus. He was shot by the gun-runner Stotz. (6R)

Sharaz Jek

JELLICOE, Arnold
The Public Relations Officer of Thinktank and secretly a member of the SRS. (4A)

JELLY BABIES
The Earth confectionery which were among those enjoyed by the Second Doctor and for which the Fourth Doctor had an especial passion.

JENKINS
One of the crew of the Edwardian sailing ship utilised by Striker in his race with his fellow Eternals. (6H)

JENKINS, Private
A UNIT soldier on duty at the raid on Devil's End to prevent the Master from succeeding in obtaining Azal's power for himself. (JJJ)

JENKINS, Steven
An immigration official at Gatwick Airport in 1966 whose body print was taken over by a Chameleon. (KK)

JENNY
A resistance fighter against the Daleks following their invasion of the Earth in 2157. (K)

JENSEN
An orderly on the planet Frontios. (6N)

JESSIE
One of the members of the Wholeweal Community based outside Llanfairfach. (TTT)

JETHRIK
A mineral, a piece of which was brought to Shur by Garron and Unstoffe and which proved to be the first segment of the Key to Time. (5A)

Jenny

JHANA BOX
A healing device developed by the Kinda. (5Y)

JIM
The fifth member of the crew of the Moonbase. (HH)

JIM
The inhabitant of the village of Devil's End who was frightened to death upon witnessing the partial release of Azal's power. (JJJ)

JIMMY
One of the reporters who came to the Ashbridge Cottage Hospital to follow up a rumour of the arrival of a man from space. (AAA)

JO
The Third Doctor received quite a shock when, totally unannounced, a petite blonde girl in a mini-skirt entered his UNIT laboratory, promptly destroyed three months' scientific work by ruining one of his experiments and then calmly announced herself as Josephine Grant, his new assistant.

Jo, with her heart set on being a secret agent, and having studied cryptology and safe-breaking, had approached an uncle of hers, who happened to be one of Britain's leading Civil Servants. She persuaded him to find her a suitable position and his display of nepotism resulted in her posting to UNIT. Her first few days with the Doctor were somewhat stormy but the arrival on Earth of the Master, coupled with a renewed invasion attempt by the Nestenes (EEE), caused him to come to accept Jo's eager-to-please manner. By the time of the incident at Devil's End she had become so much a part of the team and devoted to the Doctor that she was prepared to sacrifice herself for his sake (JJJ).

She grew to like her posting and her colleagues, but it was not until her impromptu trip to Uxarieus (HHH) that she fully realised into what fate had led her. She eventually came to terms with the fact that the Doctor was not only an alien, but was also willing to share his experiences with her. Her initial fears quickly gave way to natural curiosity and by the time she was, equally unexpectedly, transported to Peladon (MMM) she was able to accept and to adapt to new surroundings almost immediately.

Her perky cheerfulness sustained the Doctor through his constant attempts to restore the TARDIS to working order and she took his previous two selves in her stride when all three of his incarnations faced the crisis caused by Omega (RRR). She was happy for him, when at the conclusion of that adventure, the Time Lords finally restored his freedom. He shared with her the exhilaration of his renewed ability to travel in time and space.

Another aspect of life that Jo came to accept was the concept that people fell in love with her. On Earth she was dated by Mike Yates, on Peladon its king proposed to make her its queen and on Spiridon the Thal Latep begged her to return to Skaro with him. All of these she rejected and it was when she returned to Earth again that she met and fell in love with the young Nobel Prize-winning professor Clifford Jones who was to become her husband. Nepotism prevailed again when a second approach to her uncle produced the funds for a research trip for the pair up the Amazon.

Jo

There was genuine sadness in the Doctor's eyes when she announced her engagement and intention to quit UNIT to marry the young scientist, yet pleasure when she informed him that her intended husband reminded her of a younger version of himself. So his fledgling flew the coop and the Doctor showed one of his few bursts of real emotion as he realised the extent of his fondness for his diminutive assistant (TTT).

JOANNA
The sister of Richard the Lionheart, whom the English king proposed to marry to Saphadin. (P)

JOBEL
The Chief Embalmer in Tranquil Repose on Necros. He was killed by Tasambeker. (6Z)

JOCONDA
The planet which was ruled by the Doctor's friend Azmael when he left the Time Lord society, whose throne was coveted by Mestor. (6S)

JOE
A private in International Space Command posted to *Snowcap* base in 1986. He was killed by the Cybermen. (DD)

JOEY THE CLOWN
One of the opponents for Steven and Dodo in their enforced game of Blind Man's Buff in the realm of the Celestial Toymaker. (Y)

JOHN
The mineralogist on the crew of Captain Maitland's expedition to the Sense-Sphere. (G)

JOHN
The fifteenth member of the crew of the Moonbase. (HH)

JOHN
The companion to Edward Travers on his expedition to the Himalayas in 1935. He was killed by the Yeti. (NN)

JOHN, Sir
The squire in 17th century England whose manor house was taken over by the Terileptils. He and his son Charles and daughter Elizabeth were killed by them. (5X)

JOHNSON, Private
A UNIT radio technician on duty at the time of General Carrington's plot against the alien ambassadors. (CCC)

JOHNSON, Private
A UNIT soldier on duty at the time his headquarters came under siege from Omega's Gell Guards. (RRR)

THE JOKER
One of the opponents for Steven and Dodo in their enforced game of Musical Chairs in the realm of the Celestial Toymaker. (Y)

JONDAR
A rebel on Varos, who, along with his wife Areta, revolted against the system of governing there and succeeded with the help of the Sixth Doctor. (6V)

JONES
A member of the Master's coven in the village of Devil's End. (JJJ)

JONES THE MILK
The milkman in Llanfairfach. (TTT)

JONES, Clifford
A young Nobel Prize-winning professor who ran the Wholeweal Community outside Llanfairfach and to whom Jo became engaged. (TTT)

JONES, Megan
The chairperson of the Euro-Gas Corporation. (RR)

JOSH
A miner in Killingworth in the 17th century. He was made her thrall by the Rani and eventually killed by her. (6X)

JOUBERT
A member of Caven's gang of space pirates operating from the planet Lobos. (YY)

JUAN
A waiter in the *Las Cadenas* restaurant in Seville. (6W)

JULES
A Frenchman and the tenth member of the crew of the Moonbase. (HH)

JUPITER
A call sign employed by the Brigadier when UNIT was allotted the task of moving the Thunderbolt missile. (FFF)

The Joker

K

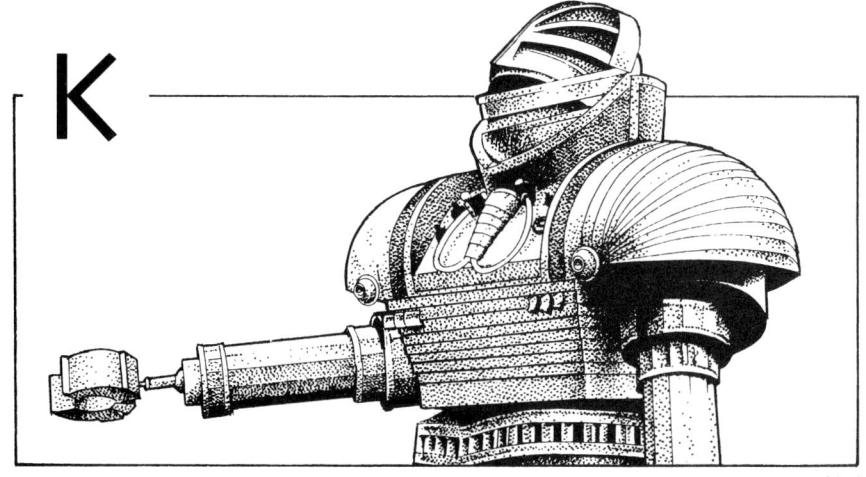

K-1

K.4067

The asteroid near Titan on which the Bi-Al Foundation was located in the year 5000. (4T)

K-1

The robot constructed by Jeremiah Kettlewell and utilised by the SRS for their own ends. It was destroyed by the Fourth Doctor using an active solution of a metal virus that its creator had also concocted. (4A)

K-9

Professor Marius built the original K–9 as his mobile personal computer in the shape of a metallic dog around the year 5000 (4T). Given into the care of the Fourth Doctor by the Professor it accompanied the Time Lord on three adventures before staying on Gallifrey with Leela (4Z). The Doctor constructed an improved Mk.II model which he proposed to take on holiday (5A) but the pair of them were sent on the quest for the segments of the Key to Time by the White Guardian, along with Romana, before he could do so. K–9 helped them in the retrieval of five of the six segments and in six more adventures before remaining in E-Space with a regenerated Romana to assist the Tharils in rebuilding their world (5S).

The Doctor also built a third model which he left as a present for Sarah-Jane to make amends for his necessary abandonment of her and it lived up to its charge of taking care of her (4N, 6K).

K-9

All models of K–9 were equipped with a defensive beam which could stun or kill and a retractable probe which permitted rapport with other machines. As a robot it was susceptible to reprogramming and on one occasion betrayed the Doctor because of the influence of the Shadow (5F). Sometimes it broke down (4X, 5J, 5N) and needed repair, on one occasion mystifyingly sustaining laryngitis (5J) which resulted in a temporary voice change (5G, 5K, 5L) which was eventually rectified. The Fourth Doctor had a strong kinship with each of the three girls who travelled with him the longest since all of them received one Mk. of K–9 when they left the TARDIS to pursue their own lives!

K'ANPO
The Abbot of the meditation centre in Mummerset. In fact he was a Time Lord and the Doctor's former teacher on Gallifrey when he was living a hermit's existence. (ZZZ)

KAFTAN
The wealthy Arabic member of the Brotherhood of Logicians who financed Eric Klieg's expedition to Telos. She was killed by the Cyber Controller. (MM)

Kaftan And The Cyber Controller

KAHN, Doctor
The assistant to Professor Kyle who was killed by the Cybermen's androids. (6B)

KAJABI INDIANS
The South American tribe that cut out the tongue of George Cranleigh and drove him insane when he discovered the Black Orchid. (6A)

KAL
The would-be usurper of the leadership of the caveman tribe which tried to learn the secret of fire from the First Doctor. He was killed in combat by Za, the man he rivalled. (A)

KALA
The wife of Aydan and a citizen in the city of Millenius on Marinus. She conspired with her husband and the court prosecutor Eyesen to have Ian convicted of murdering Eprin. (E)

KALDOR
A city on the world where the TARDIS materialised

aboard a sandminer, where a robot masseur went berserk, as mentioned by Chub. (4R)

KALEDS
The race on Skaro which eventually mutated into the Daleks as genetically engineered by Davros (4E), called Dals earlier in their history (B).

KALID
The guise adopted by the Master when he hijacked two Speedbird Concordes through time. (6C)

KALIK
The ambitious brother of President Zarb on Inter Minor. He coveted his brother's position and sought to usurp it but, caught in his own scheme, was killed by a Drashig. (PPP)

KALISTORAN
A 'bad' member of the Xeraphin life force. (6C)

KALMAR
An outlaw with scientific leanings on the planet in E-Space where the *Hydrax* was drawn by the Great Vampire. (5P)

KAMELION
A silver android with shape-shifting ability, the tool of an invader of the planet Xeriphas. It aided the escape of the Master from Xeriphas and he brought it with him to Earth (6J). It was susceptible to the will of others and it was the Fifth Doctor's will which first brought it on board the TARDIS (6J). Later the will of the Master caused it to become his slave once more and betray the Doctor before begging to be shrunk out of existence by the tissue compression eliminator (6Q). His time with the Doctor may have been short but Kamelion made an impression on him, for the Time Lord remembered him as his life ebbed away into his fifth regeneration (6R).

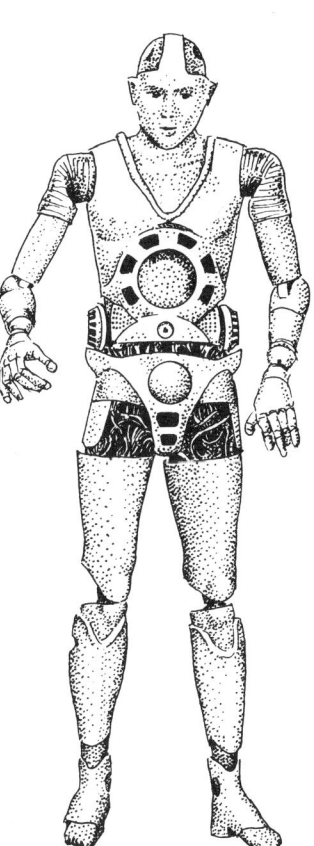

Kamelion

KAN-CHOW
A city through which the caravan of Marco Polo travelled. (D)

KANDO
A student on the planet Dulkis. She was sent to survey the Island of Death under the supervision of Educator Balan. (TT)

KANDOR
An executive grade in Megropolis Four on Pluto who falsified computer records and thus enriched himself and some fellow conspirators at the expense of the Company; he was confined in a Correction Centre in retribution and after three years' imprisonment he died, as related to Marn by Hade. (4W)

KANI, Matrona
The assistant to Crozier on Thoros Beta. She helped him with the brain transplant operation he performed on Kiv. (7B)

KANOWA
The Australian town where Salamander owned a Research Centre. (PP)

KANTRA
A planet which is a tropical paradise. Dal Garrant, a combat pilot from that planet serving in the Third Galactic Fleet, was taken prisoner by the Daleks and forced to work for them on Skaro. When he died from exhaustion and malnutrition he was buried on Skaro by his fellow captives, the ceremony being witnessed by the Fourth Doctor and Romana. (5J)

KARA
The scheming food concentrate plant owner on Necros who after cooperating with Davros hired Orcini to kill

him. When he found she had also planned to double-cross him Orcini stabbed her. (6Z)

KARAKORUM
The town, once the capital of the Mongol Empire, where Tegana planned with Acomat the latter's raid on the caravan of Marco Polo. (D)

KARELA, Madam
The vizier to the Lady Adrasta who was as schemingly ambitious and opportunist as her mistress. (5G)

KARFEL
The twin-sunned planet which the Third Doctor visited briefly with Jo when he solved a food shortage problem. It was subsequently all but enslaved by the scientist Megelon after an accident during an experiment transformed him into the Borad. The Sixth Doctor and Peri helped the Karfelons to overthrow his rule. (6Y)

KARI
A space raider who aided the Fifth Doctor on Terminus. (6G)

KARINA
A lieutenant in the crew of Sea Base Four in 2084. She was strangled by Maddox. (6L)

THE KARKUS
The super-powered hero of a cartoon strip which ran in *The Hourly Press* in 2000. He was called into being by Zoe while in the Land of Fiction. (UU)

KARL
The son of Ivo and Marta in the village on the planet in E-Space where the *Hydrax* was drawn by the Great Vampire. Taken in the Selection, he rebelled against the Three Who Rule and his death was ordered by Zargo. (5P)

The Karkus

KARLTON
Mavic Chen's Security Chief at the Guardian's headquarters building on Earth. (V)

KARN
The bleak planet on which the Sisterhood tend the Blue Flame from which is distilled the Elixir of Life and on which Mehendri Solon sought to transplant the brain of Morbius into a new body. (4K)

KARTZ
One of the professors whose experiments with time travel on Space Station Camera were monitored and investigated by the Time Lords. The Kartz-Reimer module which they developed would only work by the provision of a genetic key utilising the symbiotic nuclei of a Time Lord. (6W)

KARUNA
The Kinda child who on Panna's death absorbed all her knowledge and experience and helped the Fifth Doctor defeat the Mara on Deva Loka. (5Y)

KASHGAR VALLEY
A region in the plain of Pamir through which the caravan of Marco Polo travelled. (D)

KASSIA
One of the five consuls of the Traken Union. She was the second wife of Tremas and thus step-mother to Nyssa. She became obsessed with the Melkur and so was easy prey for the Master's hypnotic influence under which she helped him to gain the powers of the Keepership. Once she had helped him achieve this he dispensed with her life. (5T)

KASTERBORUS
The constellation in which Gallifrey is to be found. (4G, 5R)

KASTRIA
The bleak, deserted planet from which Eldrad hailed.
(4N)

KATARINA
Katarina was a Trojan slave, the handmaiden of the grim prophetess Cassandra, who had already predicted the girl's death long before she met the First Doctor.

Katarina

Her greatest characteristic was her loyalty which she zealously showed in shadowing Vicki, or Cressida as she was then known, for her mistress. She also tended to the wounds of Diomede (as she believed Steven to be) at Vicki's request. Unable to carry the wounded astronaut alone, the Doctor had no alternative but to accept Katarina's help in carrying him into the TARDIS and away from Troy.

It was Katarina's relative simplicity which allowed her to accept the ship's dimensions as a temple in which dwelt a great god, as she thought the Doctor to be. Neither could she hope to comprehend all the integral components in the Master Plan of the Daleks.

She did understand that her new lord was trying to save the lives of all the creatures in the universe. He could not be hindered in this task and thus she found the only way she could to prevent Kirksen from interfering in the struggle against the metal creatures. She may not have understood that the lever she pulled in Mavic Chen's ship would expel her and the criminal into space, but loyalty shone through once more as she fought to release herself from Kirksen's grasp as she sacrificed her life for the Doctor's cause. And so Cassandra's prophecy came true.
(U, V)

KATRYCA
The queen of the Tribe of the Free on Ravolox. She was killed by Drathro. (7A)

KATURA
One of the five consuls on Traken at the time that the Fourth Doctor fought the Master there (5T). She perished when the latter released entropy into the universe (5V).

KATZ
The shortened name of Katzin Makrig, a scientist on the planet Karfel who rebelled against the rule of the Borad. (6Y)

KAVELL
A member of the scientific elite on Skaro at the time of the creation of the Daleks, by whom he was killed. (4E)

KEAVER
An inmate at the meditation centre in Mummerset where Mike Yates stayed following his breakdown. (ZZZ)

KEBBLE
One of Bragen's band of rebels on Vulcan in 2020. He was killed by the Daleks. (EE)

KEEFAN
An ore to be found on the planet where the TARDIS materialised aboard a sandminer. (4R)

KEELER, Arnold
A botanist in the employ of Harrison Chase. He was infected by the Krynoid and mutated into a carnivorous plant. He was destroyed by bombs dropped by the Phantom Squadron. (4L)

THE KEEPER
The Keeper was the name given to the office of the

The Keeper of Traken

person granted the organising principle of universal harmony of the Traken Union. The Keepership bestowed great powers on the holder of the office, permitting the holder to draw on all the minds of the peoples in the Union. It was these powers that the Master coveted in his quest for a new body once his regenerative cycle had expired. (5T)

THE KEEPER OF THE MATRIX
The Time Lord entrusted with the responsibilities of being the custodian of a key of Rassilon which was used to give access to the Matrix. The one called as a witness at the trial of the Sixth Doctor was impersonated by the Valeyard. (7C)

THE KEEPERS
Those, including Arbitan and Darrius, who constructed the Conscience of Marinus. (E)

KELIA
A member of the Sisterhood on Karn. She was strangled by the Morbius monster. (4K)

KELLER, Emil
The alias adopted by the Master when he experimented with the mind parasite at Stangmoor Prison. (FFF)

KELLMAN, Professor
The civilian planetary surveyor, based on Nerva Beacon, who appeared to be traitorously working for the Cyber-

men. In fact he was working with Vorus against them. He was killed in a rock fall on Voga. (4D)

KELLY, Gia
The Senior Supervisor at T-Mat control in London in the 22nd century. (XX)

KELNER
The Castellan at the time of the attempted invasion of Gallifrey by the Vardans and subsequently the Sontarans with which latter race he traitorously cooperated. (4Z)

United Galactic Headquarters on Kembel

KEMBEL
The planet from which the Daleks launched their Master Plan in 4000. (T/A, V)

KEMEL
The mute Turkish wrestler employed by Theodore Maxtible against whom Jamie initially had to fight when the Daleks attempted to determine the Human Factor. He was pushed into a chasm on Skaro by a 'Dalekised' Maxtible and fell to his death. (LL)

KEMP
A lieutenant on the battleship which came to rescue cargo ship C–982 when it was looted by Ogrons. (QQQ)

KENDALL, Kenneth
A television newscaster at the time of the attempted take-over of London by WOTAN and its war machines. (BB)

KENDRON
A councillor on Karfel. He was killed by the Borad. (6Y)

KENNEDY
The butler at the Royal Scientific Club in 1966. (BB)

KENNEDY
A rogue employed by Edward Waterfield under pressure from the Daleks to steal the TARDIS from Gatwick Airport. He was exterminated by one of Waterfield's masters. (LL)

KENT, Giles
The former Deputy Security Commissioner for Europe and North Africa in the World Zones Organisation in 2030. Salamander double-crossed him in their joint scheme for world domination. He planned to use the Second Doctor's resemblance to Salamander to dispose of the latter and become World Dictator himself but was shot by the Mexican. (PP)

KERENSKY, Professor Theodor Nikolai
The foremost authority on temporal theory in the world in 1979 who was deceived into attempting to help Scaroth. When the latter had no further use for him he killed him by ageing him with the machine that Kerensky himself had developed. (5H)

KERRIL
A member of the crew of the sandminer aboard which the TARDIS materialised. He was strangled by one of the robots aboard the craft and at first its commander, Uvanov, blamed the Fourth Doctor and Leela for his death. (4R)

KETTERING, Charles
A scientist who liaised with the British government on behalf of Emil Keller. He negotiated permission to experiment with Keller's reform process on prisoners at Stangmoor Prison. He oversaw the first application of the Keller Machine and was 'drowned' by it. (FFF)

KETTLEWELL, Jeremiah P.
A research scientist at Thinktank specialising in robotics and secretly a member of the SRS. He was disintegrated accidentally by K–1, the robot he had created. (4A)

KEW GARDENS
The famous botanic centre which Peri expressed a wish to visit in the early 19th century. (6X)

KEWPER, Jacob
The innkeeper of *The Inglenook* in 17th century Cornwall and secretly one of *The Smugglers*. He was killed by the pirate Cherub. (CC)

KEY OF RASSILON
A black rod carried on ceremonial occasions by the President of the High Council, also known as the Great Key. It in fact unlocked the container of the Eye of Harmony in the Pantopticon; a replica of it was displayed in the Panopticon Museum (4P). Another, key-shaped, was the main component in the Demat gun (4Z) whilst a third, entrusted to the Keeper of the Matrix, admitted entry to the portals of the Matrix. This latter was duplicated by the Valeyard (7C).

KEY TO TIME
The perfect cube which maintains the equilibrium of Time itself and embodies a very powerful elemental force. It comprises six segments which are scattered through space and time. The White Guardian compelled the

Fourth Doctor and Romana to seek out the different pieces, all of which had the power of transmutation so that they could appear as anything. The segment guises proved to be: a piece of jethrik in the possession of the confidence artist Garron on the planet Ribos, the planet Calufrax, the Seal of the planet Diplos, part of a statue on the estate of Gracht on the planet of Tara, a holy relic swallowed by the squid-like Kroll on Delta Three and Princess Astra of Atrios. Once he and Romana had successfully completed their quest, the Doctor used the Key to restore order and equilibrium in the cosmos before dispersing the segments anew. (5A/B/C/D/E/F)

KEYS OF MARINUS
Micro-circuits for the Conscience of Marinus hidden across the planet for safe keeping by Arbitan. He despatched Sabetha his daughter, Altos and also the First Doctor, Susan, Barbara and Ian to recover them from their places of concealment. (E)

KEYSTONE COPS
The Hollywood comedy team whom the First Doctor encountered there briefly in the 1920s. (V)

KHEDON
A monk at the Detsen monastery in 1935. (NN)

KHEDRU
A monk at the Detsen monastery in 1935. (NN)

KHEPREN
A master builder in ancient Egypt. He was killed by the Daleks. (V)

KHNUM
The horned Egyptian god of fecundity mentioned by the Doctor. (JJJ)

KHRISONG

The leader of the warrior monks at the Detsen monastery in 1935. He was slain with a sword by the enthralled Songtsen. (NN)

KILBRACKEN

The scientist who developed a holograph-cloning technique which replicated from a single cell a short-lived carbon copy of the original being. The Fourth Doctor and Leela were cloned in this way. (4T)

KILLINGWORTH

The town in 19th century England outside which Lord Ravensworth's mine was situated and where the Rani experimented on some of his miners. (6X)

KILROY

A crew member on Rorvik's ship. He was killed when it exploded. (5S)

KIMBER

A passenger on the *Hyperion III* who had previously met Hallet on the planet Stella Stora. He was killed by the Vervoids. (7C)

KIMUS

The fiancé of Mula on Zanak who helped the Fourth Doctor to free his planet from the rule of Xanxia. (5B)

KINDA

The indigenous population of Deva-Loka. (5Y)

KING'S CROSS STATION

The London Underground station where Driver Evans observed a Yeti carrying the Great Intelligence's glass pyramid during the occupation of the tube system by the robots. (QQ)

KIRBY, Avon G.
A village store owner in Devesham, whose shop was duplicated on Oseidon by the Kraals. (4J)

KIRKSEN
A prisoner on the planet Desperus. He attempted to hijack Mavic Chen's space ship while it was in the First Doctor's possession and he took Katarina as a hostage while in the air-lock. He was killed when the slave girl opened the outward hatch of the air-lock and they were both sucked into airless space. (V)

KISTON
An engineer among Lytton's mercenaries. He was brought under control by Davros in 4590 and exterminated by the Daleks whilst assisting his new master. (6P)

KITCHEN BOY
One of the opponents for Steven and Dodo in their enforced game of Hunt the Thimble/Key in the realm of the Celestial Toymaker. (Y)

KITTY
The barmaid at *The Inferno* night club. (BB)

KIV
The leader of the Mentors on Thoros Beta. The Valeyard invaded the Matrix and made it appear to a court trying the Doctor that the Mentor ruler's brain was transplanted into Peri's body. (7B)

KLEGG
The sergeant to Algernon ffinch in the Redcoat army barracked at Inverness in 1745. (FF)

KLIEG, Eric
The president of the Brotherhood of Logicians who led an

Eric Klieg

expedition to Telos to seek out the Cybermen. He was killed by Toberman who had been partially cybernised. (MM)

KLIMT
A Guard on the planet which formed around the Minyan space ship, the *P7E*. He was killed when his shot directed against Herrick was reflected straight back at him. (4Y)

KLOUT
An Earth lawyer impersonated on Argolis by a member of the West Lodge Foamasi. (5N)

KNIGHT, Captain
The second-in-command of Colonel Pemberton's patrol during the Yeti occupation of the London Underground. He was killed by a blow from one of the robots. (QQ)

KNOPF, Ingmar
A Hollywood director whom the First Doctor encountered there briefly in the 1920s. (V)

KONTRON
A crystal with the property of time distortion to be found near the mouth of the Timelash on Karfel. (6Y)

KOQUILLION
The guise adopted by Bennett to intimidate Vicki on Dido. (L)

KORLANO-BETA
A world with mining operations similar to those on the planet where the TARDIS materialised aboard a sand-miner, as mentioned by the Doctor. (4R)

KOSNAX
The race which fought with the Vardans; during that war Xeriphas was devastated by crossfire. (6C)

KRAALS
The race from the planet Oseidon who attempted an invasion of Earth using androids. They had first tested the androids in a duplicate of the village of Devesham which they created on their world. (4J)

KRAIL
A cyberleader who invaded *Snowcap* base in 1986. He was shot down by General Cutler. (DD)

KRAKATOA
The volcano in the Sumatra Straits, at the eruption of which in 1883 the Doctor mentions he was present. (DDD)

KRANG
A cyberleader who invaded *Snowcap* base in 1986. He was shot down by Ben. (DD)

KRANS
One of the crew of a scout ship from Gal Sec colony stranded on Earth and forced to take part in Styre's experiments. (4B)

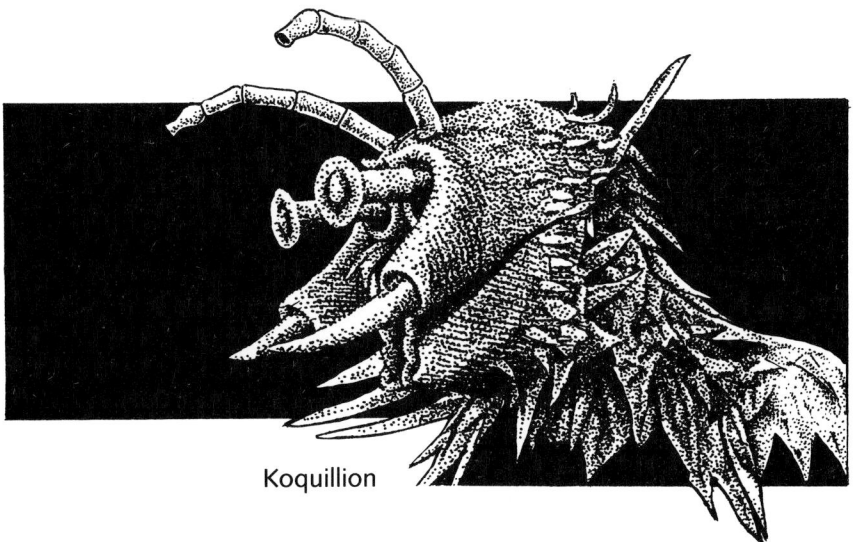

Koquillion

KRASIS
The High Priest of Atlantis at the time of the Master's attempted dominance of Kronos. (OOO)

KRAVOS
A member of the military elite on Skaro at the time of the creation of the Daleks, by whom he was killed. (4E)

KRELPER
A member of Stotz' band of gun-runners. He was shot by his leader. (6R)

KRIMPTON, Professor
The electronics expert conditioned by WOTAN into serving its planned world take-over via *The War Machines*. He was killed by the reprogrammed war machine. (BB)

KRISTAS
One of the Thal group encountered by the First Doctor on his original trip to Skaro. He accompanied Barbara, Ian, Antodus, Ganatus and Elyon on the rear offensive on the Dalek city. (B)

KRIZ
A Solonian mutant whose space craft crashed on Karn where he was killed by Condo. (4K)

KROLE
A Levithian guard in the retinue of the Graff Vynda-K. (5A)

KROLL
A blind squid-like creature which dwelt in the swamp on Delta Three. It swallowed a relic holy to the Swampies which was in fact the fifth segment of the Key to Time. This caused it to grow to enormous size. When the Fourth Doctor used the Tracer to change the relic back to the segment, Kroll was split into many tiny creatures. (5E)

KRONOS
One of the Titans of Greek legend and a chronovore – a time devourer. He was drawn into time by the priests of Atlantis by means of a crystal which became known as the Crystal of Kronos. The Master tried to harness its power through the use of TOMTIT. (OOO)

KRONTEP
A land on the planet Thordon of which Yrcanos was the king. (7B)

KROTONS
Crystalline creatures which enslaved the Gonds in order to use their brain energy to pilot their crashed space craft back to their own planet. They were destroyed when the Second Doctor had the craft and creatures attacked with a derivative of sulphuric acid. (WW)

KRYNOIDS
The creatures into which Charles Winlett and Arnold Keeler mutated after being infected by germinating plant pods from space which travelled to Earth in a pair and were preserved in the snows of Antarctica. They were both destroyed by bombs. (4L)

KUBLAI KHAN
The Mongol Emperor to whom Marco Polo intended to give the TARDIS in order to win his freedom. (D)

KUIJU
The begger hired by Tegana to steal the TARDIS and who also tricked Ping-Cho into handing over all her money. He was killed by a warrior in Ling-Tau's retinue. (D)

KURKUTJI
The Australian Aborigine collected by Monach and reduced to silicon chips, which were used to motivate an android body. He left Earth 35,000 years before the Fifth

A Krynoid

Doctor encountered him on the Urbankan spaceship. (5W)

KURSTER
The sergeant-at-arms to Count Grendel. (5D)

KY
A Solonian tribal war chief; the Doctor helped him to win his planet's independence from Earth in the 30th century during which time he mutated into the highest form of life on his world. (NNN)

KYLE, Professor
The paleontologist and geophysicist whose geological survey expedition was devastated by the Cybermen's androids. She was killed by a Cyberman. (6B)

KYLE, Sergeant
The desk officer of the police station to which Coolie was taken following the murder of Joseph Buller. (4S)

A Karfelon Android

ARTISTE APPENDIX

Virgil Earp	Victor Carin
Warren Earp	Martyn Huntley
Wyatt Earp	John Alderson
Earthling	Christopher Owen
Eckersley	Donald Gee
Captain Edal	Peter Thomas
Edith	Alethea Charlton
Edu	Edward Kelsey
Edward of Wessex	Alan Rowe
Communications Officer Edwardes	Simon Slater
Squire Edwards	Paul Whitsun-Jones
Eelek	Philip Madoc
Eirak	Martin Potter
El Akir	Walter Randall
Elders	Edmund Bailey (OOO)
	Wilfred Boyle (OOO)
	Colin Cunningham (OOO)
	Tony Douglas (AA)
	Nicholas Edwards (AA)
	Royston Farrell (AA)
	Eric Francis (G)
	Fiona Fraser (AA)
	Donald Groves (6Q)
	Lynn Howard (AA)
	Harry Lewis (6Q)
	Reg Lloyd (OOO)
	Bartlett Mullins (G)
	Peter Penny (OOO)
	Terry Randal (6Q)
	Colin Thomas (6Q)
	Christine Wass (AA)
	Lionel Wheeler (AA)
	Bill Whitehead (OOO)
Eldrad	Judith Paris and Stephen Thorne
Eldred (S)	Peter Russell
Eldred (XX)	Philip Ray
Eleanor of Wessex	June Brown

Elena	Dione Inman
Elgin	John Cannon
Mark Elgin	Tony Adams
Elizabeth	Valerie Fyfer
Elizabeth I	Vivienne Bennett
Elyon	Gerald Curtis
Engin	Erik Chitty
Enlightenment	Annie Lambert
Eprin	Dougie Dean
Erak	Peter Walshe
Erato	Tom Baker (voice)
	David Brierley (voice)
	Myra Frances (voice)
	Lalla Ward (voice)
The Ergon	Malcolm Harvey
Eric	Gordon Pitt
Erskine	Peter Roy
Etnin	Malcolm Terris
Etta	Sheila Reid
Ettis	Ralph Watson
Doctor Evans	Alan Rowe
Driver Evans	Derek Pollitt
Dai Evans	Mostyn Evans
The Examiner	Martin King
Exorse	Geoffrey Frederick
Exxilons	Leslie Bates
	Bob Blaine
	Derek Chater
	Terry Denville
	Steven Ismay
	Kevin Moran
	Roy Pierce
	Dennis Plenty
	Mike Reynel
	David Rolfe
	Terry Sartain
	Nigel Winder
Eyesen	Donald Pickering
Fabian	Helen Blatch
Faraday	Patrick Newell
Fariah	Carmen Munroe
Farrah	Paul Lavers
John Farrel	Stephen Jack
Mary Farrel	Barbara Leake
Rex Farrel	Michael Wisher

Farrow	Frank Crawshaw
Fatima	Viviane Sorrel
Federico	Jon Laurimore
Fedorin	David Nettheim
Ralph Fell	John Rolfe
Doctor Fendelman	Denis Lill
Fenner	Philip Madoc
Alastair Fergus	David Simeon
Astrid Ferrier	Mary Peach
Luigi Ferrigo	Gabor Baraker
Fewsham	Terry Scully
Algernon ffinch	Michael Elwyn
Fibuli	Andrew Robertson
Bill Filer	Paul Grist
General Finch	John Bennett
Fish People	Cathy Ash
	Derek Calder
	Nigel Clayton
	Alex Donald
	Perin Lewis
	Mary McMillan
	Judy Nicholls
	Tony Starr
Kate Fisher	Sheena Marshe
Fisk	Geoffrey Hinsliff
Hugh Fitzwilliam	Christopher Villiers
Isabella Fitzwilliam	Isla Blair
Ranulf Fitzwilliam	Frank Windsor
Sean Flannigan	James Mellor
Flash	Ewan Proctor
Flast	Faith Brown
Flavia	Dinah Sheridan
Flower	Kay Patrick
Johnny Flynn	Tony Harwood
Foamasi	David Korff
	Andrew Lane
	James Muir
Corporal Forbes	George Lee
Forester	Alan Tilvern
Duke of Forgill	John Woodnutt
Howard Foster	Dallas Adams
Fosters	Philip Bloomfield
	Maurice Connor
	Michael Gordon-Browne
	Pat Gorman
	Donald Groves

	Pat Judge
	Barney Lawrence
	Mark Midler
	Jim Morriss
	Ralph Morse
	Stuart Myers
	Liam Prendergast
	Fred Reford
	Doug Roe
	Tony Snell
	Barry Summerford
	Colin Thomas
Frankenstein Monster	John Maxim
Franz	Barry Ashton
Frax	Trevor Laird
Colin Frazer	Alastair Cumming
Froyn	Bill Meilen
Fu Peng	Khristopher Kum
Fuller	Johnny Barrs
Functionary	Stuart Fell
Fungoids	John Scott Martin
	Jack Pitt
	Ken Tyllson
Galleia	Ingrid Pitt
Galloway	William Sleigh
Dan Galloway	Duncan Lamont
Ganatus	Philip Bond
Kert Gantry	Brian Cant
Gaptooth	Jack Bligh
Gardiner	Ray Lonnen
Garge	Geoffrey Cheshire
Jaynis Garif	Alan Rowe
The Garm	R.J. Bell
Jan Garrett	Wendy Gifford
Garron	Iain Cuthbertson
Jeff Garvey	Barry Jackson
Garvin	John Joyce
Detective Inspector Gascoigne	Peter Whitaker
Gastropods	Ridgewell Hawkes
	Steve Wickham
Gazak	Steven Mackintosh
Gaztaks	Tony Allef
	Bruce Callender
	Hi Ching
	John Holland

Gearon	James Muir
Gebek	Ranjit Nakara
Gell Guards	Jack Pitt
	Rex Robinson
	Murphy Grumbar
	John Scott Martin
	Rick Newby
	Cy Town
Gentek	Mike Elles
Gern	Gregg Palmer
Gerrill	Jeremy Chandler
Gharman	Dennis Chinnery
A/B Girton	Rex Rowland
Tom Girton	Jon Croft
Giuliano	Gareth Armstrong
Sabalom Glitz	Tony Selby
Sir Keith Gold	Christopher Benjamin
Gold Usher	Maurice Quick (4P)
	Charles Morgan (4Z)
Gomer	Dennis Edwards
Gonds	Keith Ashton
	Ronnie Chance
	Roger Charles
	Justine Elliott
	Robert Hayward
	Alex Hood
	Nick Hunter
	Mark Johnson
	Patricia Matthews
	David Melbourne
	Reg Nardi
	Peter Rann
	Nick Rutter
	Robin Scott
	Sylvia Steele
	Wendy Wilson
Albert Goodge	Andrew Staines
Commandant Gorton	Richard Steele
Gotal	Roy Heymann
Goth	Bernard Horsfall
Goudry	Michael Keating
The Governor	Martin Jarvis
Grant	Michael Guest
The Gravis	John Gillett
The Great Intelligence	Wolfe Morris (voice – NN)
	Jack Watling (voice – QQ)

The Great One
Magnus Greel
Major Green
Senior Prison Officer Green
Edwin Green
Steinberger P. Green
Gregory
James Gregson
Grell
Count Grendel
Grey
Grey Lady
Solicitor Grey
Grierson
Griffin
Griffiths
Doris Griffiths
Grigory
Grogan
Percy Groom
Charles Grover
Grugger
Grun
The Guardian (HHH)
Guardians (X)

Jack Woolgar (voice – QQ)
Maureen Morris (voice)
Michael Spice
Alan Curtis
Eric Mason
Hus Levent
Royston Tickner
Ian Fairbairn
Hugh Morton
Timothy Walker
Peter Jeffrey
Ray Armstrong
Roslyn De Winter
David Garth
Dave Carter
Reg Lye
Brian Glover
Jean Burgess
Stephen Flynn
Pat Gorman
Christopher Wray
Noel Johnson
Bill Fraser
Gordon St. Clair
Norman Atkyns
Mark Allington
Andrea Beddows
Raymond Byron
Terry Cashfield
Rosemary Chalmers
Diane Chapman
Roy Douglas
Jackie Duval
Royston Farrell
Deryn Fisher
Iris Fry
George Gibbs
Hazel Graham
Paul Greenhalgh
Ron Gregory
David Greneay
Trevor Griffiths
Philip Harris
Stephanie Heeson
Bill Hunter
Paul Johnson

	Tony Kemp
	Jacqueline Lewis
	Paul Linley
	Rosemary Lord
	Sheila McGrath
	John Moyce
	Victor Munt
	Sara Negus
	Alan Norburn
	Michael Osborn
	Jackie Salt
	Judith Webb
	Gloria Williams
	Jan Williams
Guardians (4G)	Nick Burnell
	Kevin Selway
Guardoliers	Richard Bonehill
	Peter Gates Fleming
	Kevin O'Brien
	James Richardson
Lemuel Gulliver	Bernard Horsfall
Gundan	Pat Gorman
	Robert Vowles
Gunnar the Giant	Ronald Rich
Habris	Iain Rattrary
Hade	Richard Leech
Hafsa	Diane McKenzie
Hal	Jeremy Bulloch
Bob Hall	Alec Ross
Hallet	Tony Scoggo
Peter Hamilton	Julian Fox
Jane Hampden	Polly James
George Hardiman	Donald Hewlett
Hardin	Nigel Lambert
Hardy	John Rees
Harg	Grahame Mallard
Hargreaves	Seymour Green
Harker	Rio Fanning
Captain Harker	Tim Piggott-Smith
Haroun	George Little
Harper	Rudolph Walker
Seth Harper	Shane Rimmer
Frank Harris	Roy Spencer
Maggie Harris	June Murphy
Harry (JJJ)	James Snell

Harry	Ian Marter
Sergeant Hart	Richard Steel
John Hart	Edwin Richfield
Teresa Hart	Judith Lloyd
Captain Hawkins	Paul Darrow
Vince Hawkins	John Abbott
Olive Hawthorne	Damaris Hayman
Peter Haydon	Bernard Holley
Professor Hayter	Nigel Stock
Hector	Alan Haywood
Hedges	Kenneth Walker
Hedin	Michael Gough
Professor Heldorf	Gordon Sterne
Doctor Henderson	Antony Webb
Sergeant Henderson	Ray Barron
Hensell	Peter Bathurst
Hepesh	Geoffrey Toone
Nicolai Hermack	Jack May
Hermann	Kevin Flood
Herrick	Alan Lake
Heslington	Barry Wilshire
Hetra	Ian Thompson
George Hibbert	John Woodnutt
Edwin Hickman	Hugh Futcher
Hieronymus	Norman Jones
High Minister	Gladys Spencer (voice)
High Priest (XXX)	Mostyn Evans
Hilio	Martin Jarvis
Hilred	Derek Seaton
Hindle	Simon Rouse
Hinks	Ben Howard
Hippias	Aidan Murphy
Hlynia	Jocelyn Birdsall
Ho	Vincent Wong
Jack Hobson	Patrick Barr
Jim Holden	John Herrington
Doc Holliday	Anthony Jacobs
Hopkins	Michael Pinder
Captain Hopper	George Roubicek
Horg	Howard Lang
Gilbert Horner	Robin Wentworth
Clive Horton	Peter Dahlson
Horus	Gabriel Woolf (voice)
Hrhoonda	Arthur Blake
Hrostar	Arne Gordon
Huath	Kismet Delgado (voice)

Huckle	Tony Sibbald
Ted Hughes	John Scott Martin
Humker	Billy McColl
The Huntsman	David Telfer
Hur	Alethea Charlton
George Hutchinson	Denis Lill
Stuart Hyde	Ian Collier
Hyksos	Walter Randall
Ian	William Russell
'Hippo' Ibbotson	Stephen Garlick
Ibrahim	Tutte Lemkow
Ice Soldiers	Michael Allaby
	Alan James
	Peter Stenson
	Anthony Verner
Ice Warriors	Sonny Caldinez (XX)
	David Cleeve (YYY)
	Terence Denville (YYY)
	Tony Harwood (XX, ZZ)
	Alan Lenoir (YYY)
	Kevin Moran (YYY)
	Steve Peters (XX)
Icthar	Norman Comer
Idas	Norman Tipton
Idmon	Jimmy Gardner
Inga	Rachael Weaver
Ruth Ingram	Wanda Moore
The Inquisitor	Lynda Bellingham
Irongron	David Daker
Isbur	Michael Attwell
Dom Issigri	Esmond Knight
Madeleine Issigri	Lisa Daniely
Ivo	Clinton Greyn
Ixta	Ian Cullen
Izlyr	Alan Bennion
Jabel	Leon Eagles
Jack	Terry Walsh
Jacko	Paul Anil
Jackson (4Y)	James Maxwell
Jackson (6H)	Tony Caunter
Miss Jackson	Frances Pidgeon
Jaeger	George Pravda
Jagaroth	Tom Chadbon ⎫ (voices)
	Peter Halliday ⎭

Henry Gordon Jago	Christopher Benjamin
Jailer (H)	Jack Cunningham
Jall	Penny Casdagli
Jamaica	Elroy Josephs
James (TTT)	Roy Skelton
Jamie	Frazer Hines
	Hamish Wilson (UU 2–3)
Jamie's Ghost (6K)	Frazer Hines
Janet	Yolande Palfrey
Janley	Pamela Ann Davy
Jano	Frederick Jaegar
Janos	Bill Lyons
Jarl	Reg Whitehead
Jasko	Michael Mundell
Jean	Roy Herrick
Jean-Pierre	Peter Walker
Sharaz Jek	Christopher Gable
Arnold Jellicoe	Alec Linstead
Steven Jenkins	Christopher Tranchell
Jenny	Ann Davies
Jim (HH)	Ron Pinnell
Jimmy	Prentis Hancock
Jo	Katy Manning
Joanna	Jean Marsh
Jobel	Clive Swift
Jocondans	Mark Bassenger
	Graham Cole
	Les Conrad
	Mike Mungarven
	David Ransley
	Robert Smyth
	John Wilson
Joe	Alan Wells
Joey the Clown	Campbell Singer
John (G)	Stephen Dartnell
John (HH)	Arnold Chazen
Sir John	John Savident
Private Johnson (CCC)	Geoffrey Beevers
The Joker	Reg Lever
Jondar	Jason Connery
Jones	Matthew Corbett
Jones the Milk	Ray Handy
Clifford Jones	Stewart Bevan
Megan Jones	Margaret John
Josh	Nigel Johnson
Jules	Victor Pemberton

K–1	Michael Kilgariff
K–9	David Brierley (voice 5G, 5K, 5L)
	John Leeson (voice 4T–5D, 5F, 5N–5T, 5V, 6K)
K'Anpo	George Cormack
Kaftan	Shirley Cooklin
Kal	Jeremy Young
Kala	Fiona Walker
Kaleds	Michael Brinker
	Michael Bunker
	Paul Burton
	Steven Butler
	Alan Chuntz
	Peter Kodak
	Tony Long
	Peter Mantle
	Giles Melville
	Tony O'Keefe
	Richard Reeves
	George Romanov
	Ken Tracey
	Terry Walsh
Kalik	Michael Wisher
Kalmar	Arthur Hewlett
Kamelion	Gerald Flood (voice)
Kando	Felicity Gibson
Matrona Kani	Alibe Parsons
Kara	Eleanor Bron
Karela	Eileen Way
Kari	Lisa Goddard
Karina	Nitza Saul
The Karkus	Christopher Robbie
Karl	Dean Allen
Karlton	Maurice Browning
Karuna	Sarah Prince
Kassia	Sheila Ruskin
Katarina	Adrienne Hill
Katryca	Joan Sims
Katura	Margot van der Burgh
Katz	Tracy Louise Ward
Kavell	Tom Georgeson
Keaver	Andrew Staines
Kebble	Steven Scott
Arnold Keeler	Mark Jones
The Keeper	Denis Carey
The Keeper of the Matrix	James Bree

Kellman — Jeremy Wilkin
Gia Kelly — Louise Pajo
Kelner — Milton Johns
Kemel — Sonny Caldinez
Kemp — Barry Ashton
Kenneth Kendall — Kenneth Kendall
Kendron — David Ashton
Kennedy (LL) — Griffith Davis
Giles Kent — Bill Kerr
Theodor Kerensky — David Graham
Charles Kettering — Simon Locke
Jeremiah Kettlewell — Edward Burnham
Jacob Kewper — David Blake Kelly
Keystone Cops — Malcolm Leopold
— Paul Sarony
Khepren — Jeffrey Isaac
Khrisong — Norman Jones
Kimber — Arthur Hewlett
Kimus — David Warwick
Kinda — Robert Appelby
— Paul Baden
— Tobin Mahon Brown
— Chris Bradshaw
— David Cole
— Graham Cole
— Ian Ellis
— Jonathan Evans
— Laurence Ferdinand
— Charlie Gray
— Gail Griffin
— Ray Hatfield
— Paul Heasman
— Jerry Judge
— Rosalind Kendall
— Adrienne Lawrence
— Barney Lawrence
— Camilla Lawrence
— Kiki Lawrence
— Ann Lee
— Jonathan Miller
— Mike Mungarven
— Glenn Murphy
— Tim Oldroyd
— Harry Paine

	Richard Reid
	Stephen Whyment
	Alistair Wilkins
King of Hearts	Campbell Singer
Kirksen	Douglas Sheldon
Kiston	Les Grantham
Kitchen Boy	Peter Stephens
Kitty	Sandra Bryant
Kiv	Christopher Ryan
Sergeant Klegg	Peter Welch
Eric Klieg	George Pastell
Klimt	Jay Neill
Klout	Ian Talbot
Knave of Hearts	Peter Stephens
Captain Knight	Ralph Watson
Ingmar Knopf	Mark Ross
Kraal	Stuart Fell
Krail	Reg Whitehead
Krang	Harvey Brooks
Krans	Glyn Jones
Krasis	Donald Eccles
Kravos	Andrew Johns
Krelper	Roy Holder
Professor Krimpton	John Cater
Kristas	Jonathan Crane
Kriz	John Scott Martin
Kronos	Marc Boyle
Krotons	Robert Grant ⎫
	Robert La Bassiere ⎬ (bodies)
	Miles Northover ⎭
	Roy Skelton ⎫ (voices)
	Patrick Tull ⎭
Krynoid	Mark Jones (voice)
Kublai Khan	Martin Miller
Kuiju	Tutte Lemkow
Kurkutji	Illarrio Bisi Pedro
Kurster	Martin Matthews
Ky	Garrick Hagon
Professor Kyle	Clare Clifford
Sergeant Kyle	David McKail